BUILDING THE SKIFF
CABIN BOY

BUILDING THE SKIFF CABIN BOY

A Step-by-Step Pictorial Guide

by Clemens C. Kuhlig
with Ruth E. Kuhlig

Foreword by John Atkin,
the skiff's designer

International Marine Publishing Company
Camden, Maine

This book is dedicated to the best craftsman I ever knew: my father, Clemens Otto Kuhlig, whose sails have long been furled.

It is also dedicated to Ruth E. Kuhlig, whose patience and intelligence have kept the Kuhligs afloat and the old man at his bench.

Clemens C. Kuhlig

CONTENTS

ℱOREWORD

For a good many years I worked as a consultant for one of the leading yachting publications at the annual New York Boat Show. Not uncommonly, I'd be asked by people browsing through various designs, "Can I build a boat? I have a shop full of power tools." But there was often very little indication of what was available in the way of motivation! My experience has reasonably well indicated that a great many people "can build a boat"—but that I am not capable of determining this for them.

I often think of a chap named Paul Morss, from a town called Horsehead on Lake Seneca, N.Y. Mr. Morss visited me during one of the boat shows and showed me photographs of a delightful example of one of my late father's designs named *Heart's Desire*. Now the *Heart's Desire* is a complex little vessel—no plywood box or anything approaching it. Twenty-three feet overall, double-ended in form, incorporating the box keel of the Jersey Sea Bright skiff, she is not "easy to build." Mr. Morss is an accountant and the *Heart's Desire* was his *very* first attempt at turning his hand to boatbuilding—and he produced a remarkably fine piece of work.

After mulling over the idea, I don't think "anyone can build a boat." It takes a very special sort of person, someone with very special attributes—not the least of which is a world of patience—and the ability to combine the use of the hands with the use of the head. I am among the last to encourage the uninitiated to get involved in an unknown venture. And Clemens Kuhlig cautions against undertaking a project that is beyond the layman's ability when he writes, "Care should be taken in selecting the right boat for your requirements." Further, strong consideration should be given to selecting a design, even with limited judgment, that appears to be within your building capabilities—and one that will perform the desired functions. There is a lot to be said for "learning the ropes" with a boat of modest dimensions—and then proceeding to greater tasks when it is determined that the enthusiasm is maintained.

Unfortunately, it is not uncommon for the prospective builder to undertake a project far more time-consuming and involved than he had ever imagined. But then, without first-hand experience, there is really no way for the neophyte builder to determine just what *is* involved. All too often boats are started—and left unfinished when the builder becomes discouraged. My friends Bill and Pat Phillips, of Cambria, California, took seven years to build their 36-foot schooner, *Endurance*, from my design of the *Island Princess*. That is a very long time, so it is fortunate that they were just as enthused when final details were falling into place as they were when they laid the keel.

Clemens Kuhlig must be the ultimate perfectionist! Rarely does one find his quality of workmanship, or see evidence of the time and patience apparent in his work. A traditionalist by any standard, Clemens expresses his fondness for wood and natural materials—not neglecting, however, new products that he has found to be practical. Considerable detail is included in his book on how to construct suitable hand tools—that chapter in itself is most enlightening. But there are, as he mentions, some excellent tools available—made both in this country and abroad—for the prospective builder who does not feel inclined to fashion his own tools. Beyond the rudiments of small-boat construction, Clemens covers the techniques of adding inlays and other decorative details. Informative descriptions are included on the building of wooden belaying pins, cleats, blocks, and all manner of fascinating "old-fashioned"—and time-proven—equipment.

Yes, it does take a "special breed" to maintain interest in building a boat—anticipating the day of launching—and feel the tremendous reward of accomplishment all too few of us experience when that day arrives. It is obvious Clemens Kuhlig is one of this "breed."

John Atkin
Noroton, Connecticut

Chapter 1

INTRODUCTION

In these days of mass production, engineered efficiency, and white-collar workers, we are two or three generations removed from apprenticeships—watching and helping and learning from men who have spent years learning their craft. Rare is the experience nowadays of growing up in the shop, watching work being done and noting the "tricks of the trade."

In fact, the word *craftsman* is shifting in meaning from "artisan or skilled worker" to "hobbyist." As a result, home craftsmen too often rely on kits or "quick-and-easy" methods, which are short on individuality. Many times this is due merely to a lack of exposure to the techniques of careful craftsmen. In addition, even when the would-be builder has a strong desire to make a particular object, he often lacks experience in gluing and shaping and fastening, thus making the task seem too difficult. Perhaps one substitute for an apprenticeship would be a movie of a craftsman whose every move is carefully detailed. In a sense, this is what this book is, but the action has been stopped on each page and explained more thoroughly than could be done in a movie. Hopefully, these step-by-step photographs will provide a reasonable facsimile to watching a man work.

It is my purpose to present the construction of a small boat in such a way as to make the undertaking seem attainable and worthy of time and effort. Doing such work can be an enriching and satisfying experience. With the "lessons" provided here, perhaps accessories, tools, and eventually boats will be buildable by those who may never have had the opportunity to observe a craftsman at work.

1

POINTS TO CONSIDER

Before beginning any project that will involve time, skill, and money, it is necessary to count the cost. If a projected plan anticipates some of the obstacles, the chances are that the task will be completed. Whether starting a cleat or a boat, consider work space, time, materials, and tools. Generally, self-satisfaction comes from completing the task, not just starting it.

SELECTING A BOATSHOP

While the ideal boatshop would be located on the waterfront and surrounded by boats of desirable characteristics, it is possible to build a boat under less perfect conditions. If a choice *is* possible, choose a well-insulated area with wooden cross beams and a wooden floor. The warmth is needed for the curing of glues and varnishes, and the wooden beams are excellent for attaching the braces for framing up the boat. Wooden floors also seem to be more comfortable underfoot, and they are warmer than the more common concrete. Either basement or garage may be suitable to accommodate the home woodworker. A sturdy bench with a vise is a worthwhile addition, but it is possible to use clamps rather than a vise.

TIME

It was once said that the Japanese, on their overcrowded island, have always made an effort to conserve space, while Americans always try to save time. It is true that people generally have time for whatever is most valuable to them. If the desire to build and create is there, the time will be there, too. Perhaps it is time, more than any other factor, however, that will be slighted during planning. Allowance of enough time will make the difference between an acceptable job and an excellent one.

WHICH BOAT TO BUILD

Since the boat you build will involve considerable expenditure of time, both in building it and in using it, care should be taken in selecting the right boat for your requirements.

The large quantity of designs available is surprising to anyone unfamiliar with boating. Novices tend to think of a boat as a vehicle to carry them across the water. The only options seem to be a power boat or a sailboat. The more acquaintance one gains with boating and the water, the more one comprehends the need for a wide choice of designs. A boat's design reflects both its use and the owner himself. Perhaps more than any other possession, a boat is an expression of the owner's personality and values.

Several variables that are manipulated in boat-design choice are hull design, sailing rig, building materials, and fastenings, as well as the size, the characteristics of the body of water in which the boat will be used, and the kind of care the finished boat will receive. The owner must decide and weigh the importance of each factor so that the final choice actually is an expression of himself. The boat being built here, the *Cabin Boy*, exemplifies this decision-making process.

The boat we desired would be used primarily by a youngster learning to row and sail, but it would also need to be useful as a dinghy to tend a larger boat kept at a mooring. It would be used in both salt and fresh water, in areas that are generally well protected. While needing to be light enough to be carried from rack to water, the boat would also have to be stable enough to allow for errors made by a beginner learning to row and sail.

As for finishing choices, they would be varied enough to allow the youngster to learn about varnish, paint, and oiled surfaces. The boat's being beautiful would not have to be a deterrent to its being "child-proofed" by the addition of special oarlocks, simple ties for oars, and simple rigging for sailing. As for storage, the boat would be kept in a garage or outside on a rack during the winter months. Other personal requirements demanded that there be stowage space for every bit of a sailor's equipment, from life jacket to anchor, and that there be at least one brass cleat to be kept polished as evidence that the young sailor was learning the value of a well-maintained vessel.

Taking all these quite personal specifications into consideration, the design choice was a flat-bottomed rowing skiff with a sprit rig, designed by John Atkin. (The building plans and offsets for the *Cabin Boy* may be ordered from John Atkin, P.O. Box 5, Noroton, Connecticut 06820.)

NOTE: Study plans for three additional flat-bottomed boat designs by John Atkin appear in the Appendix, which begins on page 134.

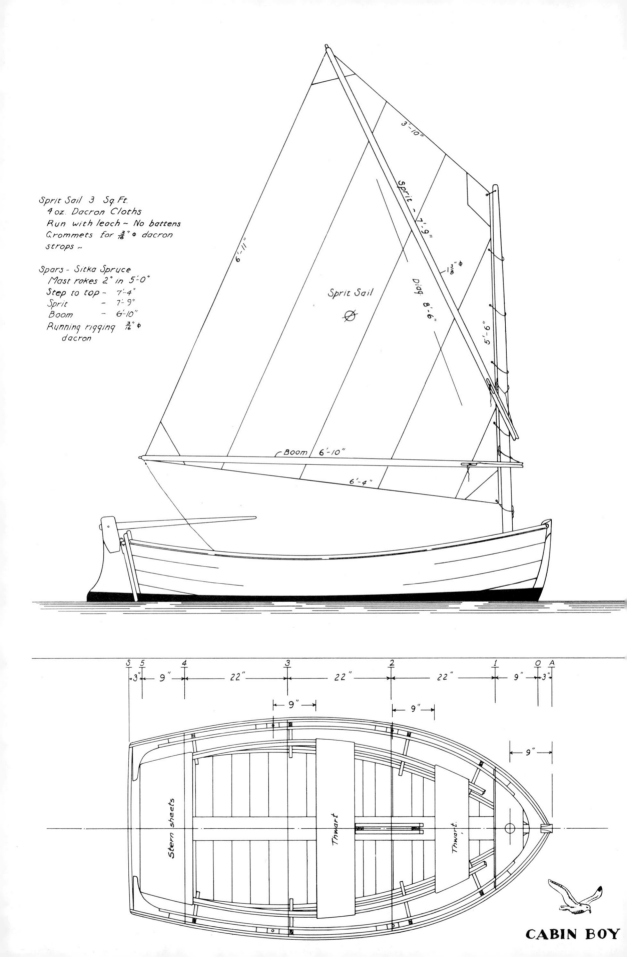

Sprit Sail 3 Sq.Ft.
  4 oz. Dacron Cloths
  Run with leach ~ No battens
  Grommets for 3/16" ⌀ dacron
  strops ~

Spars - Sitka Spruce
  Mast rakes 2° in 5'-0"
  Step to top - 7'-4"
  Sprit   - 7'-9"
  Boom   - 6'-10"
  Running rigging 3/16" ⌀
      dacron

Sprit Sail

3'-10"

Sprit ~ 7'-9"

6'-11"

Diag 8'-6"

1/8" ⌀

5'-6"

Boom 6'-10"

6'-4"

Stern sheets

Thwart

Thwart

S   5   4   3   2   1   O   A
3" 9"   22"   22"   22"   9" 3"

9"   9"

9"

CABIN BOY

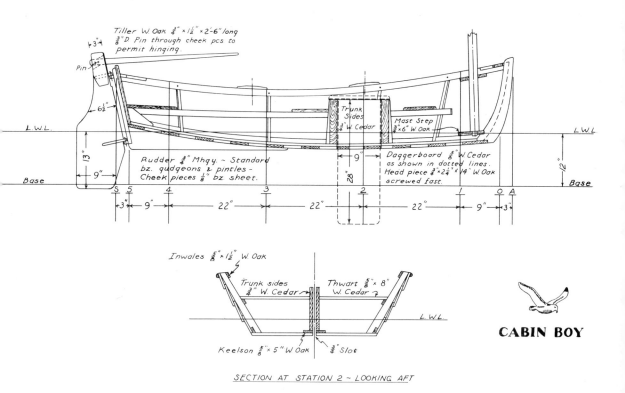

SECTION AT STATION 2 ~ LOOKING AFT

CABIN BOY

HULL DESIGN

The major factor that determined a flat-bottomed boat in this case, rather than a vee-bottomed or round-bottomed one, was its simple construction. However, it was desirable that the negative points of the flat-bottomed hull be minimized. Flat-bottomed boats are noted for pounding, but to my satisfaction, the designer made the chine lines at the bow quite narrow, thus limiting the amount of pounding. He also gave the sides flare, contributing to buoyancy, dryness, and stability while under sail—important considerations for a beginner. (The lapstrake design also helps maintain dryness by directing the spray outward.) The addition of a skeg satisfactorily lessened the probability that the craft might veer off course while rowing. Since the boat is also a tender, the skeg is an advantage when the boat is being towed or beached. It adds a dimension of protection to the hull. While flat-bottomed lapstrake was a good design choice, the size was the next consideration. Again, use was the key factor. In this case, the rowing sailboat is for a youngster, so the choice was determined finally by the size of the proposed skipper!

SAILING RIG

It is best not to change the rig the designer has specified. He has considered many factors—including weight, size, and intended use of the boat, and changing the rig is a complicated procedure. The final design choice, then, should include both hull and rig, leaving no alterations to be made by the builder.

The advantages of the spritsail are quite obvious: the spars are lightweight, they store easily in the boat, and they lack complicated rigging. For the beginner, the sprit rig is ideal, since it can be taken down easily, and the boat can be converted quickly to a rowing boat. Simple cleats and securing procedures make the rigging easy to handle for even the youngest learner. The speed and ease with which the rig can be set up facilitate taking short sails, even just sailing out to the mooring when the boat is used as a tender.

Since each design cannot be lifted from the paper and tried, and since many designs never do get built, it is impossible to say truly that one design is the "ultimate." Each sailor must determine to the best of his knowledge and his experience what will probably be the best for him. Again, it is a personal choice. When the boat does what you hoped it would do and then some, you have made a good choice.

Chapter 2

BOATBUILDING MATERIALS

One preoccupation of the modern-day boatbuilder is the selection of materials for his boat. With science and industry developing new, promising products almost annually, the choice seems very difficult. I have chosen wood as the medium I prefer for boatbuilding. The reasons for my choice are both subjective and objective. Like any personal opinion, this one has some elements so subtle that it is difficult even for me to sort them out. For example, is wood *really* more beautiful than plastic? Do the planing and sanding and varnishing *really* make the grain an object of beauty? Is it *really* "easier" to work with? Is it *really* "warmer" than plastic or metal or concrete? Perhaps some more scientific mind can prove warmth and beauty. I only know that I prefer wood.

For year-in and year-out use, wood has some advantages that are often slighted by the plastic and metal salesmen. While refinishing usually is considered an annual job to be dreaded, making the boat's beauty come alive again makes the task somewhat lighter. Also, there have been many misconceptions about painting and varnishing, and stories of painting problems have been retold and embellished by salesmen eager to downgrade the values of wood in favor of the medium they happened to be hawking.

While the disadvantages of wood are constantly brought to our attention, the qualities that have made it effective have been slighted. It is not unusual, for instance, for a person to compare a brand-new fiberglass yacht to a 40-year-old wooden boat and conclude that plastic is obviously better.

Aesthetics aside, it is still true that wood can be worked into an infinite variety of forms, and that simple tools can be used in connection with learnable skills to turn out a boat to be proud of. Both repairs and alterations of a wooden craft are possible with no special aid from a boatyard or hardware store. With the same skills the builder used to build the boat, he can embellish and repair it. Metal and plastic call for specialized tools and techniques that are not widely available.

As the final argument for the use of wood, I hold up its proven durability. New products are still being tested, but experience with wooden boats has proved that a well-built, well-maintained hull will outlast its owner. Taking into consideration availability, cost, practicality in use, proven durability, and beauty, I cast my vote for wood.

Economics must also be considered here, of course. As with time, we generally can afford whatever holds value for us. Wood, fastenings, and finishing materials are available for building a beautiful boat. It is up to the woodworker to decide whether the project is worth the investment.

When choosing woods to build your boat, it is best to follow the designer's specifications. One reason that he has chosen specific woods is that their individual qualities warrant use in certain parts of the boat and their weights are appropriate for the intended use. Too often, a builder has trouble locating certain woods, and he uses incorrect substitutes, thus changing the weight above or below the waterline. The accompanying chart shows the weight of each type of wood. If substitutes are necessary, first consider these weights.

SPECIES	WEIGHT PER CUBIC FOOT (in pounds)
Locust	48
Teak	47
White oak	47
Ash	41
Peruvian mahogany	38
Walnut	38
Hackmatack	36
Honduras mahogany	36
Cherry	35
African mahogany	32
Alaskan cedar	31
Port Orford cedar	29
Sitka spruce	28
Philippine mahogany	27
Western red cedar	23
White cedar	23

WOOD	CHARACTERISTICS	USE
Plywood* (Bruynzeel Regina)	light; strong; finishes well	rudder, daggerboard, bottom, side planking
White oak	dense; strong; durable; easily steam-bent; workable	frames, stem, keelson, skeg, tiller
White cedar	aromatic; lightweight; highly rot-resistant; easily steam-bent; swells quickly when wet	planking, seats, daggerboard trunk
Red cedar**	light; rather soft; resistant to rot; somewhat strong; easy to work; splits easily	planking, joiner work
Teak	dense; heavy; extremely durable; rot-resistant	decks, trim, gratings
Sitka spruce	light; stiff; strong in proportion to weight; little shrinking or warping in use	spars
Ash	hard; strong; shock-resistant; rot-resistant; can be used where light weight with strength is important	oars, boathooks, handles, tiller
Cherry	does not warp, shrink, or check; highly rot-resistant; tough; hard; strong; takes varnish well; gnarled growth habit makes it a good source of natural knees; not easily steam-bent	decorative work, blocks
Hackmatack	strong; heavy; close-grained; rot-resistant; a good source of natural knees	knees, stem
Locust	very strong; hard; heavy; virtually immune to rot; workable with sharp, heavy tools	bitts, mooring cleats, wedges, treenails
Walnut, black	heavy; dense; strong; varnishing brings out rich grain	interior work, blocks

---

*Do not use lumberyard varieties of exterior plywood. The stresses and strains of boat use require the highest-quality plywood. Marine-grade plywood is stronger, has more layers (plies), and is less likely to have voids.

**Western red is only one of the three main categories of cedar found on the West Coast. Each has its distinctive uses and characteristics.

WOOD	CHARACTERISTICS	USE
Mahogany		
African	reddish color; no natural rings, so it can be identified easily; beautiful, but softer, lighter, and less strong than other two true mahoganies	in veneers and plywood, can be used in interiors and for seats in small craft
Honduras	lighter than African, but heavier, harder, and stronger; straight grain takes fine finish	seats, planking, rudder, rails, other trim
Peruvian	very heavy; very dark; much tougher than other two true mahoganies; nearly impossible to split; extremely durable	(not readily available)
Philippine***	light; rot-resistant; moderately strong; warps and swells little, yet can be steam-bent; grain is coarse and open with little depth in color, making it a poor substitute for true mahogany	planking, seats

---

***This wood is *not* a true mahogany. It bears a trade name given to three different tree species comparable to cedar that are found in the Philippines. No doubt its surface resemblance to the true mahoganies led to its being called by that name. Its steam-bending qualities make it better for planking than for interior or decorative uses.

Do not use kiln-dried wood. With weather and water exposure, boat lumber must be of very high quality. The finish work will not prevent problems if improper woods are selected. If at all possible, the builder should air-dry his own lumber. A second-best solution is to deal with a reputable company that will guarantee that the proper seasoning has been completed.

METALS FOR MARINE USE

As with the wood selection, the choice of which metals to use for what purposes also offers a dilemma for some home craftsmen. Beside the accepted "traditional" metals stand the rather new alloys, which offer promise of greater corrosion resistance, the main factor to consider when choosing the metal fastenings and fittings. Corrosion, in simplest terms, is the process in which refined metals revert to their natural state, and the strain that a boat puts on fittings, as well as dampness and salt water, tend to speed the process. While steel is generally used for rigging, and bronze alloys are used for fittings, the choice of modern blends can be dazzling. Listed below are a few of the more commonly accepted and available metals and their uses.

METALS	CHARACTERISTICS	USE
Bronze alloys	includes silicon bronze, which is very corrosion-resistant	bolts, screws, fittings
Hot-dipped galvanized steel and iron	zinc coating provides excellent protection against corrosion	fastenings, fittings
Brass	soft; not to be used below waterline or in any structural capacity	decorative objects above waterline
Monel	highly recommended for stiffness and corrosion resistance	fastenings, fittings
Stainless steel	best used alone; the bedding on another metal can hasten deterioration	wire rope, fastenings, fittings
Copper	soft; flexible; highly resistant to corrosion	rivets for fastening hull

Chapter 3

TOOLS FOR BOATBUILDING

Tools for boatbuilding can be bought or made, depending on the desires and pocketbook of the builder. There are many tools available, and it is recommended that care be exercised before making a purchase. As a rule, I have found that so-called combination tools and gadgets are not desirable. Each job has a correct tool for doing a job efficiently. It is the workman's choice as to which tool will serve him best. I have also noted that many people do not choose a tool to fit themselves; rather, they consider only the job to be done. When selecting hand tools especially, consider the handles as well as the "tool." Will it truly be an extension of your arm and hand? Does your grip cramp your hand? Are the handles long enough to accommodate the shaft? Mass-produced tools aim for the average person and often overlook individual needs. As a result, some tools that will be used over and over may be better made by the worker to fit himself exactly. For that reason, plans for planes, bow saw, and bow drill are included. These three tools are used often enough to be worth making.

POWER TOOLS VS. HAND TOOLS

Three basic tools for boatbuilding are the saw, the sander, and the drill. A table saw with blades for ripping and crosscutting saves time and energy, but it is possible to do without this power tool. Contrary to magazine and television advertisements, hand saws can rip and crosscut quite effectively. A power sander is a help, but a circular sander is to be avoided because of the undesirable circular marks it leaves on the wood's surface. A straight-line sander is the best choice. Again, hand sanding is possible, and sometimes it is the *only* way to get a handsome finish. For planking a hull, a power drill is extremely helpful. Again, it should be the decision of the workman, not the influence of advertisements, that determines which tools are "needed." It is his decision whether the price and usefulness of the power tool warrant its purchase.

SAWS

For crosscutting and ripping, either a power saw or hand saws may be used. For joiner work, a fine-toothed saw, such as a dovetail saw, is used. The bow saw, handmade as a replacement for the usual carpenter's saw, is advantageous to the boatbuilder. With an easily replaceable band-saw blade, plank curves can be cut without binding. The tension and angle of the blade are adjustable, and the blade retains its shape in use. As a bonus, the workman's back remains straight while he uses the bow saw, making the work less tiring. Rather than requiring sharpening after use, the band-saw blade may simply be replaced. Also, a variety of blade sizes can be purchased economically.

If you are interested in making your own bow saw, use Figures 3-1 and 3-2. While each workman may have a certain way to make a certain part, every bow-saw maker must account for tension adjustment and blade attachment, in addition to making a comfortable handle for the saw's intended use. Making an exact copy of a saw used by an eighteenth- or nineteenth-century workman is not the object here. I constructed this saw strictly for my own use in my shop. Although I copied the basic design of old bow saws and the traditional practice of labeling the saw with my initial and the date of construction, I did not make a replica of an antique saw made in another shop.

A SIMPLE SANDER

A sander that can replace a power version is pictured in Figure 3-3. The block provides a convenient grip and tends to make the back-and-forth motion more even. Holding sandpaper with just your hand may make uneven marks, which in turn will have to be leveled for a good finish.

Figure 3-1. The spindle between the bow saw's arms can be turned easily and secured quickly with the sliding wooden piece. The oak "bow," while flexible enough for tension adjustment, serves as a brace. The handles that hold the blade turn so that the blade angle is adjustable. The stainless-steel rods inserted in the handles are secured so that the blade turns when the handles turn. The nub that holds the blade is shaped with a metal file.

Figure 3-2. The proportions for the bow saw's arm, handle, and spindle. Note that the spindle has a copper nail driven through the center to hold the wooden piece.

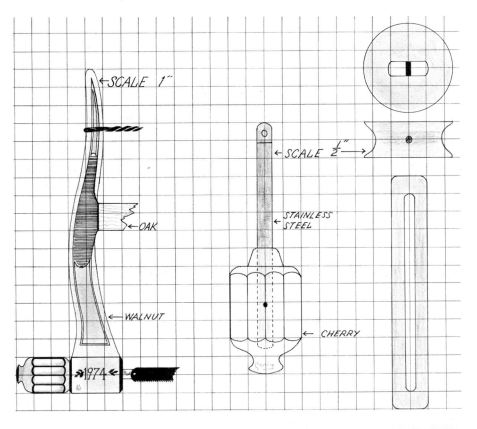

Figure 3-3. A useful sander is made by cutting a block of wood to a size appropriate to the sandpaper most often used. After the back end of the paper is set and the block is pushed backward into it, the front edge of the paper is inserted and wedged to keep it taut.

DRILLS

Pictures of the brace and the bow drill (Figures 3-4 through 3-7) are included not only to show some alternatives to the purchased variety, but also to show more possibilities of toolmaking, which are limited only by the imagination.

Figure 3-4. The brace, made entirely of wood, features a replaceable bit and a sturdy handle.

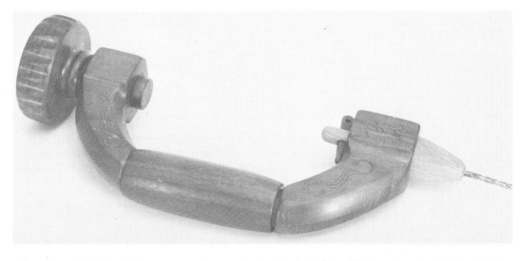

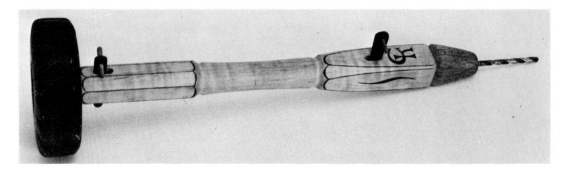

Figure 3-5. The bow drill is very practical: it can be carried anywhere and can even be used on a boat with little difficulty. The wedged handle and bit placement make it very storable, yet it is used easily. The bits are the same size as those used in the brace (see Figure 3-4), so they may be inserted in either tool. The bits are secured in the wooden chucks with molten lead.

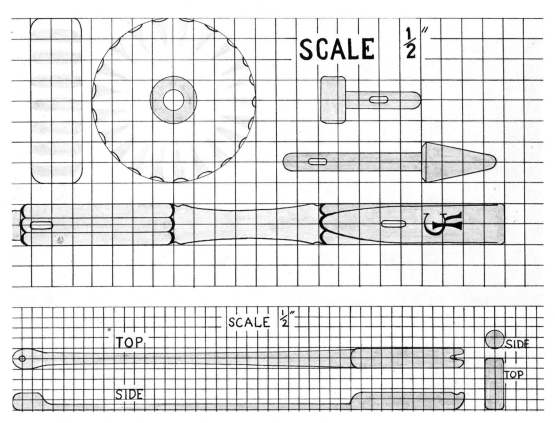

Figure 3-6. The scale drawing indicates the appropriate sizes for each part. While specifications for the bow are given here, it should actually be rather wide to begin with and then shaped as the tool is used, eventually delivering the tension leeway desired.

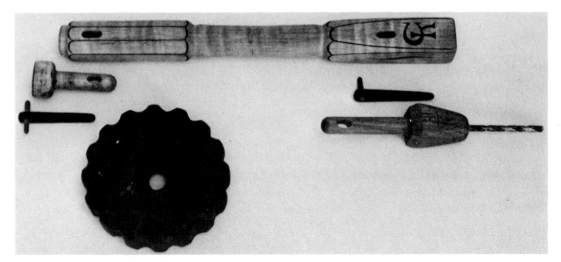

Figure 3-7. The components of the bow drill.

PLANES, DRAWKNIVES, AND SPOKESHAVES

Three types of planes are very desirable for the serious woodworker: block plane, smoothing plane, and long jointer. Two other useful shaping tools are the drawknife and the spokeshave. The drawknife roughly shapes large timbers and speeds the process of "taking down" the wood. The spokeshave is excellent for shaping spars and other rounded surfaces and warrants purchase if boatbuilding is to be done.

Discussions of the merits of metal and wooden planes can be endless. In my experience, wooden planes have proved superior. Two factors that cannot be disputed are that the wooden soles are replaceable and the plane itself is resilient, should it fall from a bench or other work surface. Not so objectively, I also consider the touch of the wooden surface to be more acceptable; the wooden surface seems to glide over the work in a much gentler way than the metal plane. Also, I prefer the wedge adjustment of the blade. While to the novice the wedge seems troublesome, practice makes it simple. Again, the tool should be an extension of the man, and his tools should help, not hinder, his work. Whether metal or wood, power or hand, the tool should be the means to a fine job, one worthy of pride.

The block plane is perhaps the best one to construct first. While it offers an introduction to basic plane construction, it also is a tool that is used often. After making and using the block plane, you will be able to determine whether other planes may be necessary for your shop.

The block plane's four parts are shown in Figures 3-8 and 3-9. To make the plane, follow these steps.

Step 1: By using two separate pieces of wood, you can cut a hole that will allow ample room for both iron and shaving. After being satisfied that the hole is wide enough to receive the iron, glue the two sides together.

Step 2: The shoe is attached by countersinking screws and plugging them. The plane will wear with use, so if the shoe is not made, then the wedge and iron would have to be readjusted to the new size of the plane. If the shoe is attached, the wood can be replaced, keeping the plane useful without changing its size.

Step 3: Shaping the wedge is important, because it must be very gradual to allow for blade-cut adjustment. Note also that the wedge is quite long, reaching nearly to the blade's edge. I have discovered that this extra length makes the double iron unnecessary. The wedge keeps the blade where it is adjusted, and it also keeps the blade from "chattering" along the surfaces planed.

According to historians who have collected information about the work habits and tools of our forebears, it was not uncommon to find many planes in the shop of the early craftsman. In fact, many woodworkers may have had as many as 50 or 60 planes, each with a special purpose. While that number might be out of the question for the home woodworker, there are several additional planes that are very helpful for the boatbuilder (Figures 3-10 through 3-19).

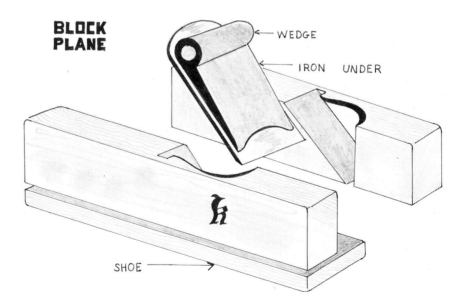

Figure 3-8. A sketch of the block plane shows the body, shoe, iron, and wedge.

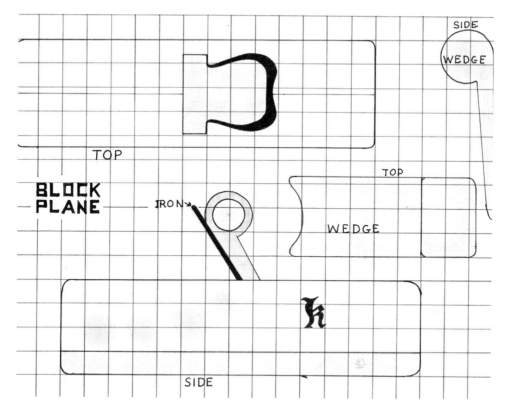

Figure 3-9. In this drawing of the block plane's parts, each square represents 1/2".

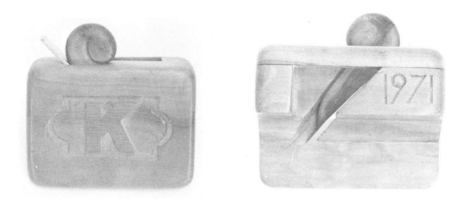

Figure 3-10 (left). The molding plane is used to put an edge on a seat or a rail. Its 45-degree cutting angle is determined by the iron and the opening made. The plane is only 3" long, just enough for a sure grip. Figure 3-11 (right). The opposite side of the molding plane shows the angle to be cut. Notice the length of the wedge.

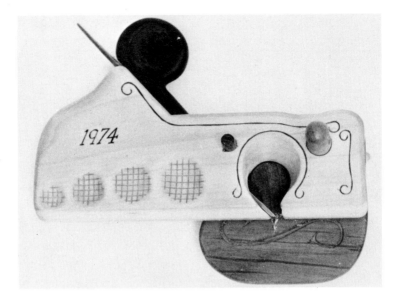

Figure 3-12. This tongue plane was designed for planking a lapstrake boat. With modern bedding compounds such as Life-Calk, it is desirable to have a gasket that allows for the swelling and shrinking of the material. This plane puts a groove in the plank at the lap. The cut is 1/8" wide, a measurement determined by the iron size. The fence, which guides the plane, is adjusted here for use from right to left.

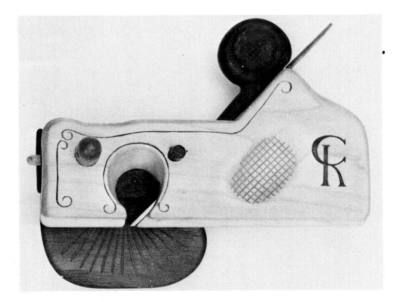

Figure 3-13. The tongue plane's fence is adjusted for cutting a groove from left to right.

Figure 3-14. The rabbet plane is another useful implement for boat-building. For small craft, the 1" iron is practical, and the fence attachment makes the size and location of the cut variable. Like the tongue plane, the rabbet plane can be used in either direction, depending on placement of the fence.

Figure 3-15. A bird's-eye view shows the rabbet plane's fence extended outward, with the wedges securing the "arms."

Figure 3-16. The fence has now been moved quite close to the cutting blade of the iron.

Figure 3-17. The rabbet plane has notches on its arms to aid in the selection of the correct placement and proper alignment of the arms.

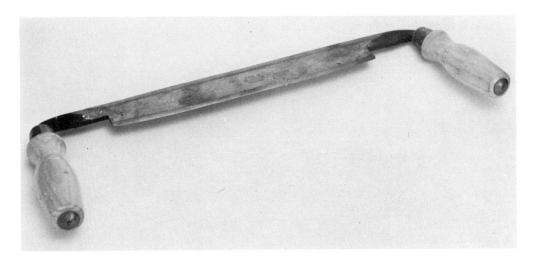

Figure 3-18. The drawknife, a kind of plane, can be used efficiently for taking down large timbers, preparing them for final shaping.

Figure 3-19. The spokeshave is good for rounding surfaces and for planing areas that may be difficult to reach with a common plane.

SCREWDRIVERS

Screwdrivers manufactured for use with wood screws are different from the standard hardware-store variety. The difference is in the finish of the tip used to turn the screw. Most conventional models have a beveled edge, which may slip from the head, stripping the slot and marring the wood. The square-cut tip is much easier and more efficient to use. Choosing the proper tip is only part of choosing the right screwdriver.

Again, a screwdriver is used so often that consideration of the handle's shape and the material from which it is made is also important. Too often, fine-quality shafts and points are fitted with too-small round handles made of breakable plastic. To grip a screwdriver, the handle must be large enough to accommodate your hand and have a shape that contributes to your ability to hold it properly. Consider the whole tool before buying it.

CHISELS AND CARVER'S TOOLS

Various sets of chisels of differing quality are available. I recommend that the woodworker choose individual tools to perform a specific task rather than purchase a whole set of chisels or carver's tools. When the need for more variety is evident, then consider handles and the quality of shaft materials, as with screwdrivers.

RIVETING TOOLS

For riveting, a drill, nippers, holding (or backing) iron, and a ball-peen hammer are necessary (Figure 3-20). The nippers must be strong enough to cut a copper nail, and the hammer must be sized to the nail being used for riveting.

The backing iron can be made by pouring molten lead into an aluminum beer can into which a ⅜-inch stainless-steel rod has been placed. The tip of the rod is then shaped to the size of the nail head used. A covering of either leather or canvas keeps hands from becoming dirty from the lead and also protects the planking if the "iron" is dropped while in use.

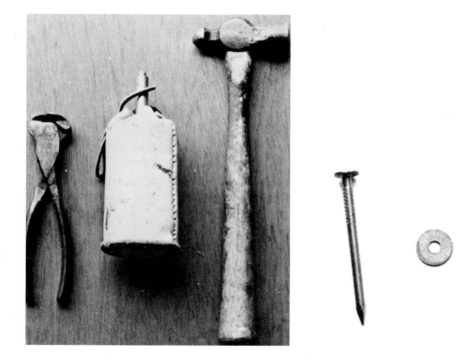

Figure 3-20 (left). The tools used for riveting: nippers, backing or holding iron, ball-peen hammer. The hammer allows the circular movement necessary for tripping over the nail and onto the burr; the backing iron keeps the nail head in place; the nippers cuts the nail close to the burr. Figure 3-21 (right). Round-headed copper nail and burr.

SHARPENING STONE AND MALLET

While a saw can be power or hand operated, a sharpening stone (Figure 3-22) for a hand tool must be used by hand. A fine, hard, Arkansas stone gives the final, razor-sharp edge to chisel, plane blade, or carver's tool. A high-speed power grinder causes the metal to lose its temper, and the result is disastrous! A mallet is essential when you use carver's tools.

Figure 3-22. A sharpening stone. This essential implement should be stored in a place where dust cannot collect on its surface. A box serves this purpose well and protects the stone from accidental dropping, which may break it.

Figure 3-23. A personalized sharpening-stone box. Long ago it was the custom for a craftsman to place his mark on everything in his shop. As the home craftsman becomes more skilled, he can understand readily the reason for this practice. Not only does this make the woodworker especially proud of his tools and materials, but as he makes and personalizes his own tools, he furthers his knowledge of his basic material, wood.

Figure 3-24. A hardwood mallet is another useful boatbuilding tool. A mallet is a must with carving tools: the wooden head is kind to handles and the weight is not so great that it tires the user or applies extra pressure on the wood being worked.

COMPASS

The compass pictured here (Figures 3-25 through 3-29) was made for use in transferring the lines of the boat to the full-size plans. Since it is used specifically for that task, the arms of the compass must be made of hardwood, and the points and arc must be sturdy enough to be used with confidence. The transfer of the lines is crucial and must be done extremely carefully. The materials needed are:

WOOD

Arms

two pieces	white oak or other hardwood	⅝" x ⅝" x 21½"

Nuts

two pieces	hardwood such as walnut	¾" x 1⅛"

Arc

one piece	plywood or hardwood	¼" x 6" x 14"

Wedge

one piece	hardwood	⁵⁄₁₆" x ½" x 1½"
one piece	hardwood	⅛" round x 1¼"

METAL

Swivel	brass or stainless-steel pin, 2 washers, and 1 cotter ring	¼" x 1"
Hinge	brass or stainless-steel plates	⅛" x 1⅛" x 2"
	4 copper nails with burrs	
Point	awl point or stainless-steel point	5" x ⅛"

Figure 3-25. Overall view of the compass used for transferring lines. The four parts that need to be constructed are the hinge, the arc and swivel, the wedge, and the ends to which the point and pencil are to be attached.

Figure 3-26. Copper nails are riveted through the brass (or stainless) plate onto the arms. The placement of three on one arm strengthens that side; the single nail on the other arm allows the compass to function.

Figure 3-27. A pin with washer and cotter ring allows the wooden arc to move when the arm of the compass is being extended. The oblong hole in the movable arm allows use of a wedge to secure a given adjustment.

Figure 3-28. The wedge shown in the foreground is placed in the oblong hole in the movable arm of the compass to allow the user to secure a selected adjustment.

Figure 3-29. The point and pencil holders. Using the same wedge principle to secure the point and pencil, cut slots in the ends of the arms. Since the ends are tapered, the inner side of each round wooden "nut" is also tapered. The threads of the awl point help hold it securely in the hole drilled to receive it, but a stainless-steel point may be used instead and scored similarly.

STORING TOOLS

Having selected and perhaps made fine tools to work with, the craftsman must store them properly. The fine points and edges of screwdrivers, chisels, and drill bits need to be protected. If they are allowed to clatter in a drawer or are left at the side of the bench, they not only are mislaid when it is time for use, but they also wear unnecessarily.

It is educational and rewarding to make your own tools, so try your hand at making at least one before closing the subject.

Fine hand tools can also be selected at the Woodcraft Supply

Corporation, 313 Montvale Avenue, Woburn, Massachusetts 01801. Besides carrying an excellent selection, this firm has books available on specific uses of tools and their care. For the woodworker, Woodcraft's catalog is a worthy addition to the shop library.

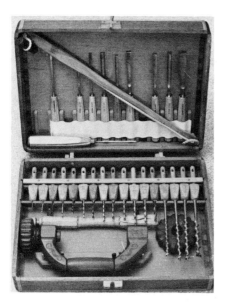

Figure 3-30. One method for storing tools in a shop. The box pictured has hinges that separate, making it possible to carry either the drills (in the bottom) or the carving tools (top) to the work area. Leather pockets for the carving-tool handles protect their points. Wooden pieces keep handles from shifting. The bow portion of the bow drill fits snugly in the box. The light wood that holds the bits is attached so that the rack of bits can be tilted upward, allowing for easy selection. The wedges used for both brace and bow drill serve a double purpose by being used to hold the brace in place during storage. The shaft and handle of the bow drill fit neatly under the drill bits.

Figure 3-31. A fitting cover for a boatbuilder's tool box incorporates several woods inlaid to depict a scene of nostalgia. The woods were selected because their grains reflected the patterns needed for rock and water, ship and sail.

Chapter 4

FROM PLANS TO PLYWOOD

"Have you lofted the plans yet?"

This is the question the experienced boatbuilder asks the novice. Not only does that question include the inference that the beginner can read and transcribe plans from small scale to full size, but it also reveals whether or not the would-be builder is serious.

There are, of course, many armchair builders. We have all met them. There are those looking for the perfect boat, the ones looking for a specific long-lost traditional design, and there are those who have found *the* boat and are planning someday to build it. But one task that separates the dreamers from the builders is the lofting. The completion of this job indicates a genuine interest in following through with the transformation from lumber pile to boat.

The lofting is done to check measurements and to provide full-size patterns for stem and transom and forms. In addition to the rather technical purposes, however, another one is almost equally important: with each measurement and point marked, with each placement of a batten, with each curve drawn, a builder is gradually and intimately introduced to the boat he has chosen to build. By the time the lofting is complete, his mind and, more important, his hands have assimilated the designer's idea, and the boat begins to take on a personality.

When the amateur looks at drawings showing the fair lines and the graceful curves of his future boat, the question that arises is a basic one: how do those curves get from the plans to my craft? The task of lofting the lines is mechanical; it is exacting rather than creative.

In the plans, there are three views of the boat. The *profile* is the view from the side. The *half-breadth* drawing is the view upward from the keel. The *body plan* consists of two half-views, one from forward and one from aft. The profile drawing shows the curves of the buttock lines against a grid of horizontal waterlines and vertical sections; the half-breadth plan shows the curves of the waterlines against a grid of horizontal buttock lines and vertical sections; and the body plan shows the curves of the sections against a grid of horizontal waterlines and vertical buttock lines.

The table of offsets is a most valuable chart, since it gives the distances from horizontal and/or vertical base lines to the curved portions of the boat. When there is no table, the measurements usually are given directly on the plans (see Figure 4-12).

Accuracy in lofting cannot be overemphasized. A small mistake on page-size plans can cause unwanted bulges and humps. They can be avoided easily if care is taken. Wrinkles and stretched or shrunken paper can distort a carefully drawn plan. For that reason, plywood is recommended as the surface for the full-size lofted drawings. The three plans can be drawn on one piece of plywood.

MATERIALS

The materials needed to loft the plans are:

Plywood: There should be enough to accommodate the actual length of the boat. A 4' x 8' sheet is enough for the *Cabin Boy*. It should be ¼" thick, flat, and smooth on one side.

Battens: Battens are thin strips of wood cut from your stock. They must be straight, uniform, and knot-free. Their sizes depend on the curves they are to form. The ones used for the *Cabin Boy* were: ⅝" x ⅝" x 9' cedar, for sheer and chine; ³⁄₁₆" x ¼" x 4 ' oak, for the stem.

Compass: The compass used in this chapter was handmade, and its details are shown in Chapter 3. If you purchase a compass, it should be rather large, it should adjust easily, it should hold its setting when in use, and it should be capable of holding a suitable drawing instrument.

Level

String

Finish nails

Thin marking pens: Three colors may be used to differentiate the three views. Choose pens that will not vary in width of mark, as that may distort the full-size plan.

Straightedge (or use a level)

Accurate ruler

Table of offsets or complete designer's plans

LOFTING THE PLANS

The steps in lofting the plans are:
  (1) Assemble materials.
  (2) Mount plywood on wall. For a small boat, nailing the plywood to a wall makes the task easier than working on the floor.
  (3) Draw profile:
    base line
    load waterline (LWL)
    floor line (construction base line)
    station lines
    sheer
    chine
    stem
    transom
    skeg
  (4) Draw half-breadths:
    sheer
    chine
    transom
  (5) Draw body plan:
    sections at stations 1 to 5 for form construction

DRAWING THE PROFILE

Since it is essential to all of the plans, the base line must be drawn with special care. (Although the *Cabin Boy* is built upside-down, all her lines are drawn on the plywood right-side up.) Near the bottom edge of the plywood, stretch a string the total length of the plywood just off the surface. If the string is kept free of the surface, there is no chance of snagging it or forcing it out of line unintentionally. Using a fine pen, as shown in Figure 4-1, mark a point at *every inch* directly under the string. Connect the points with a straightedge (Figure 4-2). Consulting the table of offsets and using the same technique of marking *every inch*, measure the distance from the base line to the load waterline (LWL) and connect the marks. Measure from the base line up to the floor line (the construction base line) and connect the marks (Figure 4-3). Measure on all three lines where the station lines should cross. Confirm these very important vertical lines by making bisecting curves with the compass (Figure 4-4). Mark each station; the profile should look like Figure 4-5 at this point. Referring to the table of offsets or the measurements shown on the plans for the sheer, measure downward from the floor line to a point on each station. These points determine the sheer line. After each station is marked, use a batten to check the curve. (Use small finish nails on either side of the batten. The batten is held firmly between the nails so that the sheer line can be drawn along it.) Before using the batten as a guide to connect the points of the sheer line, be sure to step back and assess the curve (Figure 4-6). The batten will reveal any mistake in the measurement of the sheer. Do not draw the sheer until it proves to be a "fair curve." While it is not usual for designers' measurements to be inaccurately recorded or for builders' measurements to be inexact, such mistakes have been made, and they should be corrected now. A hump in the sheer will not "work itself out"; the curve must be measured and faired. After being satisfied that the sheer is indeed as the designer planned, connect the points.

Next, measuring from the floor line down, mark each point of the chine, use the batten to check the curve, and draw the chine (Figure 4-7).

The stem's curve is next. Using the intersection of the sheer line and station A as a starting point, follow the measurements given by the designer. Mark, check with the batten, and draw the stem (Figures 4-8 and 4-9). (Figure 4-9 shows an example of stem markings, but the measurements given are not for any particular boat; they are for demonstration purposes only.) The transom and skeg are marked into the profile as shown in Figure 4-10.

Figure 4-1. A string indicates where the base line will be drawn on the plywood. Marks must be made at 1" intervals along the string.

Figure 4-2. The points of the base line are connected with a level (a straightedge will do).

FLOOR LINE

L.W.L.

BASE LINE

Figure 4-3. The load waterline and the floor line (construction base line) have been determined by measuring upward from the base line, marked at 1" intervals, and connected as shown in Figure 4-2.

Figure 4-4. The vertical station lines are confirmed with a compass.

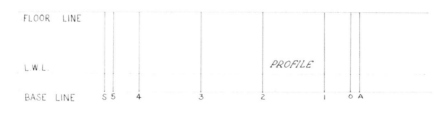

Figure 4-5. The profile with all station lines drawn.

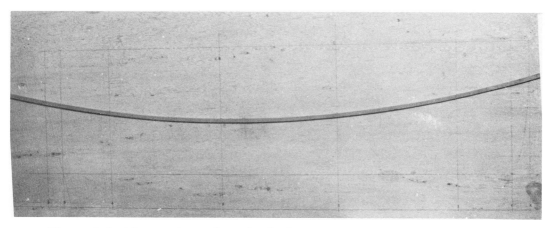

Figure 4-6. A batten is used to check the curve of the sheer.

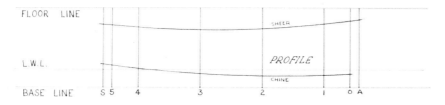

Figure 4-7. The profile now includes the curves of chine and sheer.

Figure 4-8. The curve of the stem is checked with a batten.

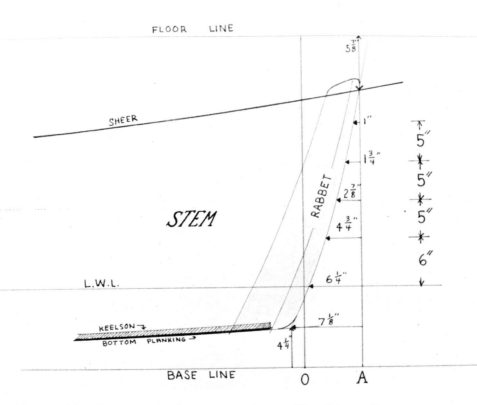

Figure 4-9. *The stem is drawn into the profile. (Note: Stem measurements indicated here are hypothetical.)*

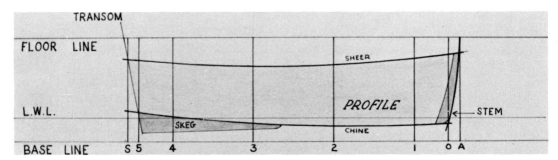

Figure 4-10. *The transom and skeg are marked on the profile.*

DRAWING THE HALF-BREADTHS

The half-breadth plan is drawn to show the angle at which the side planking meets the stem and to check the measurements given from the centerline to the sheer and chine.

There are various ways to check the angle of the stem rabbet, and in the construction of the *Cabin Boy* I chose to cut the rabbet while planking. However, the body plan still contributes to the builder's understanding of the critical point at which the side planking meets the stem. The centerline-to-sheer and centerline-to-chine measurements are crucial, so it is necessary, when lofting this plan, to note the thickness of the planking and to determine whether the designer is giving measurements from the centerline to the *inside* of the planking or the *outside* of the planking. Again, mark each station, check with the batten, and draw the sheer, chine, and transom (Figure 4-11).

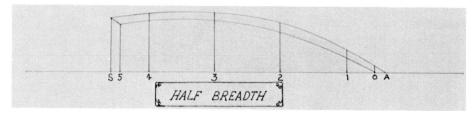

Figure 4-11. The complete half-breadth, showing sheer, chine, and transom.

DRAWING THE BODY PLAN

The body plan gives the shape of the forms at each station. Using Figure 4-12's hypothetical table of offsets, the body plan is given for station 3. Figure 4-13 shows how each of the three plans can be arranged together. Only station 3 of the body plan is shown. The half-breadth plan projects downward from the base line to show more clearly the plan's dependence on the base line. Figure 4-14 shows the profile, transom, and station 3 transferred to plywood.

After the plans are lofted and the measurements checked carefully, construction of the forms can begin.

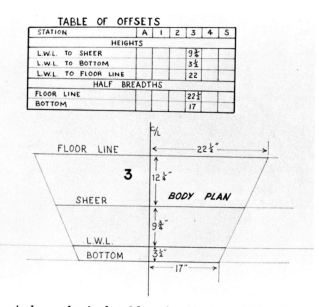

Figure 4-12. A hypothetical table of offsets, which gives only the measurements at station 3. Below it is the body plan for station 3, showing each of the measurements specified in the table.

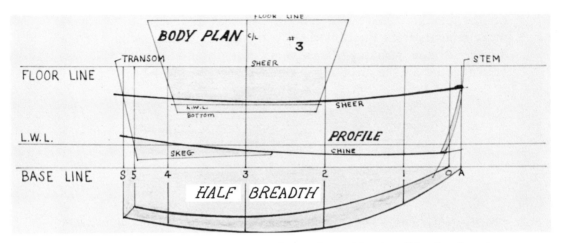

Figure 4-13. Arrangement of the three plans. To simplify the drawing, the complete body plan was not included.

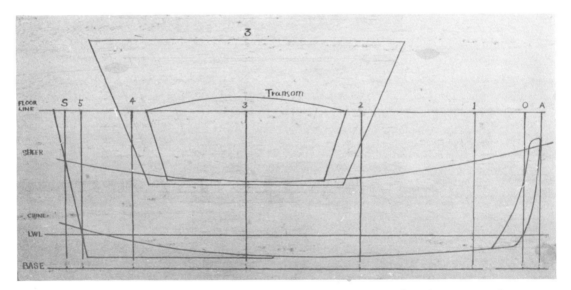

Figure 4-14. The profile marked on the plywood. Also shown are the outline of the transom and the outline of station 3.

Chapter 5

BUILDING THE BOAT

With the full-size plans drawn on the plywood, the forms can be constructed directly on these drawings.

Using one-by-six pine (or whatever is available in that size), cut the boards to make the forms, put them on the plywood coincident to the drawings, and tack them so that their accuracy can be checked. At this point, be sure to notice whether or not the measurements on the plans include the planking thickness. If they do, the width and depth of the shape produced by the body-plan forms must be reduced by the thickness of the planking. In the case of our boat, $\frac{7}{16}$ inch was subtracted from each side and $\frac{3}{8}$ inch from the bottom.

After the forms are tacked into place (Figure 5-1), draw the sheer line on the forms. Next, place a one-by-six board on the line that represents the bottom of the boat, and a two-by-four on the floor line. As before, tack both boards directly in place on the forms, and mark the centerlines on these two horizontal pieces. Always keep in mind that the boat is being built upside-down. While the one-by-six piece that indicates the bottom of the boat may be attached to the forms with four screws, the two-by-four must be removed from the forms, re-aligned, and screwed to the forms from the opposite side.

Each form is constructed from the body plan in this way: sides are placed, sheer line is marked on side pieces, bottom and floor lines are positioned, centerline is marked, and, finally, each member is secured with screws.

In Figure 5-3, the transom is shown with a frame constructed around its edges. While the designer may not call for this addition, it is recommended for two purposes: to add strength to the transom, and to provide a place to attach the chine pieces and planking, without having to screw into the end grain of the transom piece. The transom and its frame must be beveled along the upper inner edge (bottom of the boat) to accommodate the bottom piece; bevels are also made for the chine pieces and keelson.

After the forms are completed, attention can be turned to assembly of the boat's stem, transom, and daggerboard trunk before it is time to construct the building frame.

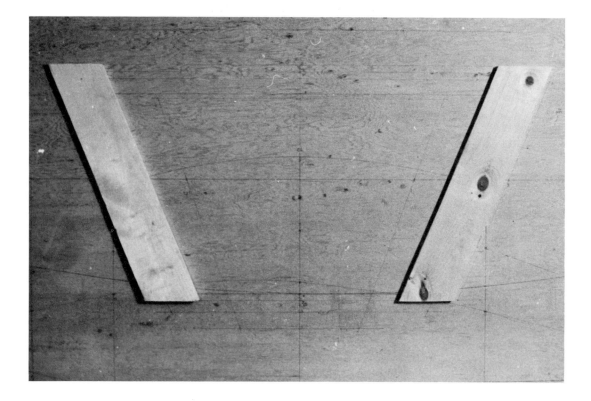

Figure 5-1. Forms can be constructed directly on the plywood plans and temporarily tacked into position.

Figure 5-2. One completed form is inverted, the position in which the Cabin Boy *will be built.*

Figure 5-3. The final form is the one for the transom, and it is shown here edged with a frame. The frame bears markings for the chines and keelson.

MAKING THE STEM

The stem of the skiff is very important. By its very nature, a skiff gets more than its share of bumps. Most designers specify an ample piece of hardwood, such as white oak, for this important member. But the builder has a choice for the construction of the stem. While laminations *can* be stronger in some cases than a solid piece of wood, the strength comes from the adhesion of the glue and the internal soundness of the bond. It is better to have the first practice with lamination on the tiller or another part of the boat where a weak or opened seam will not cause major repair work. (See laminating instructions in Chapter 6.)

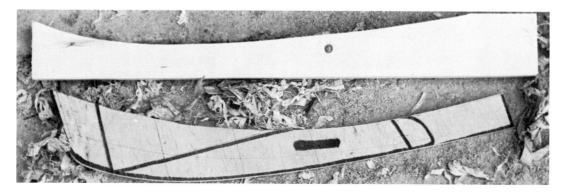

Figure 5-4. The plywood pattern for the stem, plus an additional form cut from scrap lumber. The extra piece is used to maintain the curve of the stem while it is being made (see Figure 5-6).

Figure 5-5. Eleven planed and tapered pieces of oak and African mahogany are clamped securely. Equal pressure and an ample amount of glue are needed for a strong bond.

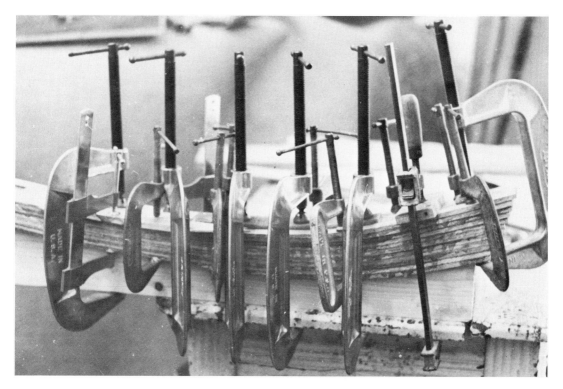

Figure 5-6. The form clamped to the stem pieces determines the final curve of the stem.

Figure 5-7. The finished stem is smoothed by planing and sanding. The notch is determined during the drawing of the full-size plans, and it allows for the keelson and the bottom piece. If the thickness of the keelson is 1/2" and the bottom piece is 3/8", the notch must be 7/8" deep.

MAKING THE TRANSOM

It is a pleasure to be able to use one piece of mahogany that is wide enough (in this case, 14 inches) for the transom. It is not impossible, however, to dowel and join narrower boards with epoxy glue. If you use the narrower boards, be sure to allow extra wood for later shaping.

First plane the rough lumber (Figure 5-8). While planing can be done at the lumberyard, hand planing is an excellent way for the builder to become acquainted with the pattern of the grain and to contemplate the effective use of its beauty.

Then mark the centerline, sheer line, and crown on the smoothed board (Figure 5-9). The crown in this case rises two inches above the sheer, at its highest point, and its curve is checked with a batten during the process of planing its top edge.

At this point, the builder should decide on any decoration of the transom. If an inlay is to be used, letters and figures can be made more easily now than on the finished boat. Remember, when planning a boat name for a transom, that there will be an oak strip to which the rudder will be "pintled," and that letters should be arranged to accommodate this piece (Figure 5-10). Chapter 6 offers guidance for making inlays.

Figure 5-8. The smoothing plane transforms rough lumber into a beautiful surface, ready to be used as the transom.

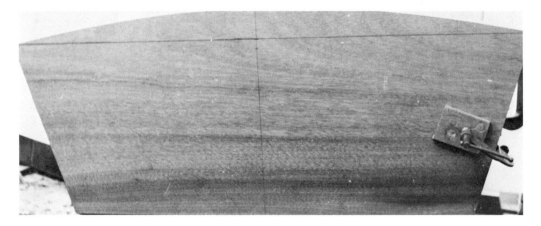

Figure 5-9. The smoothed board is marked clearly for centerline, sheer line, and crown.

Figure 5-10. A view of the finished boat shows the inlaid figure and letters. Inlays are best done as soon as the transom has been planed, although advance inlay work can mean that insufficient allowance is made for the gudgeon pad.

BUILDING THE DAGGERBOARD TRUNK

Using the designer's specifications for measurements and woods, construct the daggerboard trunk. The *Cabin Boy* has a western red cedar trunk. Although it is rather simple, the daggerboard trunk is a crucial part of the boat. It can be the source of leaks if it is not well constructed. The construction of the trunk will acquaint you with the use of Life-Calk to make the seams around the daggerboard trunk watertight (Figure 5-12). Life-Calk—manufactured by Boatlife, Inc., Hicksville, New York—is a fine example of the blending of old and new in boat construction. It is "elastomeric," which means that it moves with the swelling and the shrinking of the wood. This is an important feature for a dinghy, which in normal use is alternately dry and wet. It should be noted, however, that these modern materials cannot make up for poor fitting; it is essential that wood be planed and sanded carefully and that each piece fit precisely. Life-Calk needs no priming, except when used on oily woods, such as teak. (The manufacturer makes a primer for this purpose.) Life-Calk is easy to apply with a tube or canister and is available in white, mahogany, and black, so that colors can be matched or contrasted at the builder's discretion. I used black for the *Cabin Boy.*

As with all materials, there is a need for experience with a new medium before a builder feels confident using it. A "dry run" of the assembly should be made *before* Life-Calk application. This practice run eliminates the problem of movement of the pieces while the compound is in place. It is hard enough to line up the pieces without having to start screw holes.

After the final assembly, the screw holes are countersunk for later filling with plugs dipped in Pettit's two-part epoxy glue. Again, a high-quality epoxy glue is useful for the modern-day Noah. The plugs should be cut carefully, dipped in the epoxy, and tapped gently into place (Figure 5-14). Pettit's epoxy cuts down on the possibility of water getting at the skiff's fastenings. It is a fine product that is widely available.

The complete trunk shown in Figure 5-14 includes a trunk log. It measures 1 inch by 3 inches by the length of the trunk. While many designers do not specify the use of a trunk log for a boat this size, I think it makes sense. With the log, eight flathead bolts may be used to attach the trunk to the keelson. Screws are more apt to work loose than bolts. In so doing, they cause troubles that are not easily remedied. Bolts are more secure to begin with, and they can be replaced without an inordinate amount of work.

The trunk log should be cut a couple of inches deeper than its finished dimension so that later a handy method of establishing its exact curvature can be used to fit the keelson along its bottom edge. This method will be explained in the section on Making the Skeg, where it also applies.

Leave the daggerboard trunk at this stage of completion until after the keelson is laid. At that point, the opening can be marked and cut. The curve of the trunk log must be marked on the bottom piece and keelson at that time to secure a tight fit. The trunk is bedded in Life-Calk when it is installed so the bolts can be removed if necessary.

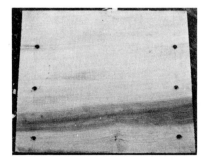

Figure 5-11. One side of the daggerboard trunk. Lines are drawn and screw holes placed before final assembly begins.

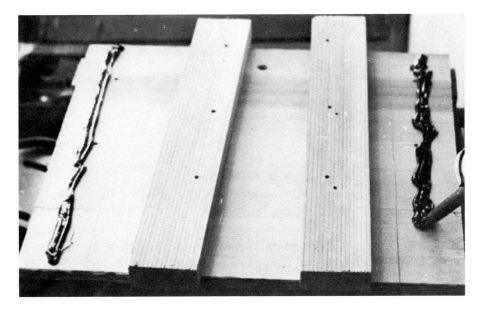

Figure 5-12. The inside of the daggerboard trunk. To allow ample room for the vertical movement of the daggerboard, the distance between spacing boards is greater than the width of the eventual daggerboard.

Figure 5-13 (left). The order of assembly of the daggerboard trunk: center screws are screwed in first, then the remaining ones. Figure 5-14 (right). The daggerboard trunk, with trunk log along the bottom. The plugs have been dipped in epoxy.

MAKING THE BUILDING FRAME

With forms, transom, stem, and daggerboard trunk constructed, it is time to start assembling the crucial building frame. The kind of floor surface available determines the amount of care needed to be taken here. The frame must provide a square and level surface for the boat's construction.

Two-by-fours are used to make the building frame and the cross members correspond to the station lines, including the transom, of the boat. These cross members are attached with screws or bolts that will hold securely when the planks are bent onto the forms. Cross members that are forward of the widest part of the boat are placed abaft the station measurement, while cross members that correspond to station lines abaft the widest point are placed forward of the station marks.

Note: Later, when the forms are being prepared to receive the planking, they must be beveled. This beveling must not destroy the correct width at each station line, so it is the forward edges of the forward forms that must be beveled. The after forms will be beveled on the after edges. If the cross members are placed properly now, the later beveling will not distort the measurement given for each station.

After construction, the building frame is checked with a level to ensure evenness (Figure 5-15). If the floor or frame is not level, nail small pieces of wood for shims wherever needed.

Figure 5-15. The building frame, made with two-by-fours, must be checked with a level. Note the station markings along the sides and the centerline marking on each station cross member.

ERECTING THE FORMS, FASTENING THE BOTTOM

Next arrange the forms on top of the frame (Figure 5-16).

Since the bottom piece of this boat runs flush across the outside of the keelson, the keelson must be placed in notches marked and cut into the forms. Lay the keelson directly on the forms, mark its width and depth, remove it and notch the forms, then replace it (Figure 5-17).

Now the notched stem (Figure 5-18) can be attached to the keelson. Attach the top of the stem to the forward two-by-four of the building frame and fit the keelson into the stem's notch (Figure 5-19). Remember that, even though there is a perfect fit, all surfaces must be bedded in Life-Calk as they are screwed into place. When satisfied with the fit of the keelson to the stem, bed and bolt it into place with a flathead bolt long enough to go through the stem (Figure 5-20). It is countersunk ⅛ inch into the keelson. This hole may be plugged later, when the boat is turned over and the excess length of the stem is also cut.

The transom is now attached to the aftermost building-frame cross member. The keelson is screwed into the frame, without making any holes in the mahogany transom.

Clamp the chine pieces into place, the forms (including the transom and its frame) having been beveled to receive them. Bed the chine pieces at the stem and transom, secure them with screws, and remove the clamps.

Notice that the width of the chine piece does not allow for the screws to be placed abreast. They are staggered so that one fastens to the stem and two are driven into the keelson (Figure 5-21). The chine pieces must fit very closely to the keelson and stem. Again, do not attempt to cover up a poor fitting job with bedding compound. Pieces must meet precisely. At the transom, a double clamping procedure is necessary because the transom must not be forced out of alignment (Figure 5-22). (If no clamp of the required spread is available, a piece of scrap lumber nailed to the form and the transom frame will also serve to keep the transom from being forced out of line.) The other clamp, as shown, holds the chine into its notched place on the transom frame.

Since the chine is at the bottom of the boat, and since the bottom piece must fit flush against the keelson and the chine pieces, a planing job is in order. Carefully move from one side of the boat to the other to avoid taking down one piece more than necessary (Figure 5-23). Check the work often with a level (Figure 5-24). Secure in the knowledge that the pieces are flat, lay the plywood for the bottom on the keelson, go underneath the boat and roughly sketch out the size, and cut along the lines marked. The bottom is not cut to fit at this point. Extra plywood must be left for exact fitting of the bottom later. By using clamps, temporarily place the bottom piece on the boat (Figure 5-25). At this point, it is a good idea to figure out the placement of the screws and, in fact, screw them in. Keep in mind the thickness of the bottom piece when countersinking. On our boat, the "dry-run" countersinking depth was about 1/16 inch. When the bottom is put in place, the screw holes should line up, and there will be a minimum of shifting on the bedding compound.

After all the screws are placed in the bottom piece, remove them and apply the Life-Calk. Replace the bottom piece and screw it into place. This time, add an extra turn of the screws, so that they are countersunk about 1/8 inch. Dip the plugs in Pettit's two-part epoxy glue and tap them gently into each screw hole (Figure 5-26). The high quality of the epoxy glue makes the plugs secure without further effort. Letting the plugs dry is an important step. After they are thoroughly dry, trim the plugs with a chisel.

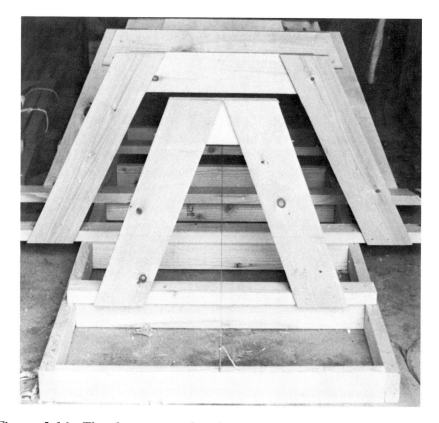

Figure 5-16. The forms are placed on top of the building frame. A plumb bob and a small line nailed to the building frame help ensure accuracy. This nail-line arrangement also assists with centering stem and keelson.

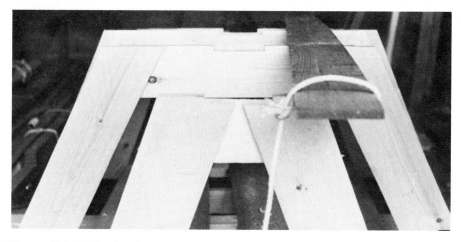

Figure 5-17. The keelson rests beside the forms notched to receive it.

Figure 5-18. The notched stem.

Figure 5-19. The stem is attached to the keelson, which is trimmed to an angle to receive the chine pieces (one chine piece is shown in position).

Figure 5-20. On the "underside" is the bolt that has been inserted through keelson and stem.

Figure 5-21. The chine pieces are bedded and screwed into the keelson.

Figure 5-22. The chine is double clamped at the transom.

Figure 5-23 (left). Chine pieces are planed to prepare them to take the bottom piece. Figure 5-24 (below). Frequent use of a level ensures the evenness of chine and keelson.

Figure 5-25. Clamps temporarily hold the bottom piece in place so the placement of screws can be determined.

Figure 5-26. Epoxy secures the plugs in the bottom piece.

MAKING THE SKEG

Cut the skeg as directed in the plans, but allow extra depth. Then, as shown in Figure 5-27, place a small but manageable block of wood under a marking pen and slide it along the bottom. In this way, the *exact* curve is transferred to the skeg for cutting. Of course the extra depth originally allowed must exceed or at least be equal to the thickness of the wooden block. Once the curve has been cut into the edge of the skeg that will fit against the bottom, then the straight edge of the skeg can be planed so the finished piece will have the correct depth. This same procedure is used to transfer the curve of the inside of the keelson to the daggerboard trunk log.

An oak stiffener is then placed down the center of the transom (Figure 5-28). This serves as a base for the attachment of the gudgeons for the rudder, and it must be at least an inch wide. By extending the oak strip below the bottom so that it can be attached to the skeg, movement of the skeg is reduced. The skeg is fastened with screws, through keelson and bottom, from the inside of the boat and to the oak strip (Figure 5-29). The long screws are all countersunk and plugged. As usual, use bedding compound wherever pieces meet or wherever wood is penetrated by a fastener.

Figure 5-27. Transfer the curve of the bottom piece to the skeg by moving a small piece of wood and a marking pen along the curve.

Figure 5-28. The oak stiffener is attached to the transom before the skeg is secured.

Figure 5-29. The skeg is bedded and screwed securely from the inside of the boat.

MEASURING FOR PLANK WIDTH

During the planking, the final look of the bow (Figure 5-30) must be planned for carefully and carried out deliberately. For example, although the planks all appear to be the same width, they are not. As the design specifies, the garboard plank is a little wider than the others. In order to accommodate the wider plank, two kinds of measurements must be taken. First, measure the total distance from the sheer to the bottom at the transom, the stem, and the center form. Divide these measurements by four. This gives the "starting point" for the plank widths. Add a little extra to this starting width to make the garboard wider. This is where the artistry comes in in boatbuilding. While no exact figure can be given, on a boat the size of the *Cabin Boy*, ¾ inch to one inch can be added to the width of the garboard. To figure the width of the remaining planks, measure the distance from the sheer to the edge of the garboard plank's rabbet. Divide this total by three (the number of planks remaining). In this way, the area occupied by the enlarged garboard is taken into account. Remember to consider rubrail width and the plank overlaps when measuring each plank. Also, since the boat has a curved sheer, the measurements *must* be taken at the stem, the transom, and the center form.

Figure 5-30. A view of the finished bow shows the following: the planks all appear to be the same width, although they are not; each plank has the same lap; there is a flush fit and a smooth, molded appearance at the stem. Preparations for these features must be well planned before planking begins, as described in the text.

PLANK AND STEM RABBETS

Two factors enter into the exact fit at the stem: the amount of wood removed from the tapered rabbets at the plank ends, and the stem-rabbet measurement. The plank's rabbet is about half the thickness of the plank where it meets the stem. Thus, when two planks are overlapped, the space taken up at the stem (and transom) is no thicker than one plank.

The stem rabbet may be cut according to the designer's plans, or it may be cut as each plank is fitted. The latter method was used in the *Cabin Boy*'s construction. A batten the same thickness as the planking is clamped to the forms. This provides the builder with a "model" plank, which demonstrates the way the plank will meet the stem. The depth of the stem rabbet and the angle at which the plank will meet the stem are considered carefully before any cutting is started. The stem rabbet can be cut with a well-sharpened chisel and a scraper. Obviously, extreme care must be taken with this procedure.

The stem is given its final molded appearance after all the planks are installed.

Figure 5-31 shows the primary step of the planking procedure. The square edge of each form must be beveled so that the planking fits flush against it. There must be no high spots protruding on the chine piece.

Now, using the width and thickness measurements of the garboard plank as the guide, cut the stem rabbet. In Figures 5-32 and 5-33 note that: the stem rabbet is cut evenly; there is an outgauge of approximately ⅛ inch to allow for the bedding compound and the swelling of the plank; the rabbet is cut for only one plank at a time.

It is helpful to have a small piece of wood that has been cut from the planking material to test in the stem rabbet as it is cut. The final rabbet should then be perfect, and the planks should fit into the stem precisely (see Figure 5-30).

Figure 5-31. Before planking can start, the forms must be beveled.

Figure 5-32 (left). The stem rabbet has been cut to receive the garboard plank. The edge of the fourth piece of the laminated stem has been used as the guideline for cutting. Figure 5-33 (below). The stem rabbet is enlarged to accommodate the entire garboard plank.

CUTTING THE PLANK RABBETS

Using a rabbet plane or a fine-toothed saw and a chisel, cut rabbets in the plank ends in order to make the planks fit flush at the stem and transom. Cut two rabbets on the outside of the lower edge (remember that the boat is being built upside-down) of the garboard planks—one at the stem and one at the stern. Cut four rabbets in the middle planks—two on the inside upper edges to lap the garboard and two on the outside lower edges to prepare for plank number three. The sheer plank, in this case the fourth plank, also has only two rabbets, this time on the inside upper edges.

The taper of the planks from the flush fit at the stem to the overlap of the full thickness of the planking material about 18 inches back from the stem is achieved by making the rabbet in the plank edge gradually shallower, from half the thickness of the planking at the stem to nothing about 18 inches abaft the stem (Figures 5-34 and 5-35).

Some boatbuilders also recommend that a small groove be made in the plank edges at this time to serve as a gasket for any excess caulking material. However, I feel that this extra step is unnecessary. By using Life-Calk on our boat, which has been subjected to fresh and salt water, the usual trailering experiences, and both heated and cold winter storage, I have found no need for such a gasket.

Figure 5-34. A rabbet plane is used to make a plank rabbet.

Figure 5-35. The plank rabbet is tapered toward the center of the plank.

TRANSFERRING THE CURVE OF THE BOTTOM PIECE
TO THE GARBOARD PLANKS

Tools needed to transfer the curve of the bottom piece to the garboard planks are: a compass, a spiling batten, a batten, and clamps. It should be noted that this is only one successful method; there are others.

The compass should be one that will not lose its adjustment, for it is important that the arc not be lost during the operation. A spiling batten may be cut from the plywood used for the lofting of the plans. It should be about five inches wide.

Clamp the spiling batten to the forms so that it is not twisted or forced in any way, thus maintaining its normal shape and preventing an edge set. Using the compass, mark the spiling batten with arcs, working from the top edge of the bottom piece (Figure 5-36). In Figure 5-37, the arcs are transferred to one of the garboard planks. The plank may be laid flat on the workshop floor for this process. It is best to avoid including the sapwood (outer edges of the plank) in the finished plank when marking off its shape. These edges are softer than the heartwood and more apt to rot.

When the highest points of the arcs are connected by a smooth curve, that line should match perfectly the curve of the bottom. The plank width measurements previously established are now made at the stem, center form, and transom in order to determine the exact size of the garboard plank. The plank now can be cut and rabbeted.

Now sand the rabbeted garboard plank on all surfaces. This practice proves helpful to the later finishing. Also, before attaching the plank, transfer the curve of the lower edge of the garboard (in its upside-down position) to the second plank (Figures 5-38 and 5-39). This eliminates further use of the compass-spiling method used above. The plank is bedded in Life-Calk at the stem, along the chine, and at the transom, and then it is screwed into place.

After the garboard plank is attached, it must be further prepared to receive the second plank. In order to have the planking maintain the proper curve that the designer planned for the hull, the lower outer edge of the garboard plank must be beveled. First the plank is spotted—notched with a saw to the correct depth specified by the design. Then a straightedge is used to check the curve (Figure 5-40). Then the plank is planed.

Figure 5-36. To transfer the curve of the bottom piece to the garboard plank, a spiling batten first is clamped to the forms, and a compass is then used to make arcs that will establish the curve of the bottom on the batten.

Figure 5-37. The arcs as they appear on the spiling batten.

Figure 5-38. The compass procedure is repeated, this time from spiling batten (on which the arcs have been connected) to the garboard plank. The arcs on the garboard plank are then connected.

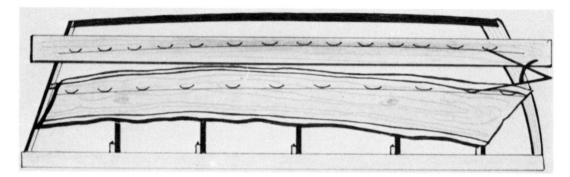

Figure 5-39. Arcs on both spiling batten and garboard plank have been connected, thus transferring the curve of the bottom to the garboard plank.

Figure 5-40. A straightedge is used as a guide to determine the amount of beveling needed on the lower edge of the garboard plank for fitting the second plank.

THE RIVETING PROCESS

The remaining planks may be fastened in a number of ways. Some of the more common fasteners are bolts, screws, cut rivets, and round rivets. Bolting, although satisfactory, may add excessive weight and lend a rather cumbersome appearance to a boat of this size. I have seen screws used to fasten laps, with the points filed smooth. This procedure seems to work satisfactorily. Silicon bronze screws are recommended if you wish to use this method. Square-headed copper nails are often recommended for planking; their selling point is that they hold better and are somewhat stronger than the round-headed nails. Round-headed copper nails were used on the *Cabin Boy* to avoid having nails on the plank's surface. Again, experience has shown that while copper nails are acceptable on the surface of the boat, they can cause discoloration of paint, so they require a filler. Countersinking and plugging of the holes is an alternative solution. With modern epoxy glues, such as Pettit's, the plugs may be set in at a depth of only $\frac{1}{16}$ inch and still hold. This results in a fine, smooth hull and a minimum of problems with finishing. Figures 5-41 through 5-47 show the riveting process.

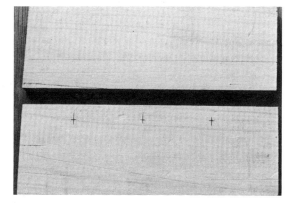

Figure 5-41. Two pieces of planking material are marked for riveting: the line on the upper board indicates the lap; the crosses on the lower board indicate the placement of the rivets.

Figure 5-42. The countersink attachment of an electric drill is used to make the holes at the cross marks.

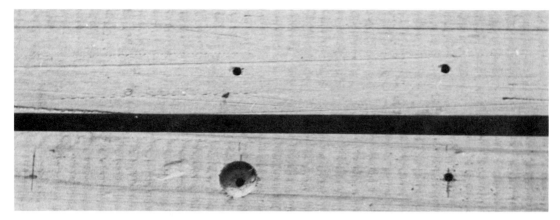

Figure 5-43. Several holes have been drilled in the planking material. The countersink attachment has been used to enlarge one of the holes.

Figure 5-44. Burrs have been placed on the nails.

Figure 5-45. A nippers is used to cut a nail close to its burr.

Figure 5-46. A ball-peen hammer is used in a gentle, circular motion to "draw up" the nail gradually. The holding iron is kept securely on the head of the nail during this process.

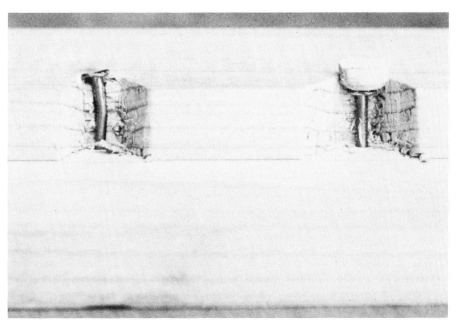

Figure 5-47. In this cutaway view, the rivet on the left shows the internal result of drawing-up strokes that were too hard. When this happens, no amount of pounding will make the plank fit tightly. On the right, however, the properly fastened rivet holds the planks together tightly and takes a plug neatly.

RIVETING THE PLANKS

The garboard plank has now been screwed into place and the lower outer edge has been beveled. The second plank has been cut out and sanded, and the laps have been marked, along with the markings for the rivets.

The plank is clamped into place with oak strips under the clamps that act as cushions and also distribute the pressure equally along the board. As usual, Life-Calk has been applied to the lapped area and also at stem and transom (Figure 5-48).

Figure 5-50 shows the evenness of the rivets on either side of the boat and the alignment of the screws into the stem.

In preparation for turning the boat over, secure the forms by inserting screws through the sheer plank into each of the forms from the outside of the sheer where the rubrail will be attached later (Figure 5-51). This will ensure that the hull does not lose its shape when it is turned over. In order to install the boat's frames, though, the forms must be removed. To maintain the hull's shape when forms are removed, use thwartships braces, screwed into place along the sheer right across the boat from sheer plank to sheer plank (Figure 5-52).

PLUGGING THE PLANKING

Since the countersinking of the planking rivets was somewhat shallow ($\frac{1}{16}$ inch), the boat must be propped up for plugging so the plugs don't fall out. Each hole has a plug carefully dipped in Pettit's epoxy glue and laid in place (Figure 5-53). Allow at least a 24-hour drying period. Chisel the protruding tips flush with the boat's surface. The resulting surface may be either varnished or painted successfully.

Figure 5-48. Planking is clamped into position, rivet holes have been drilled, and the board is bedded at the lap.

Figure 5-49. Rivets are applied from the stem toward the transom. The clamps are readjusted after each rivet is finished in order to maintain evenness of pressure and a tight fit.

Figure 5-50. Planking is complete.

Figure 5-51. The boat has been turned over, after screws were inserted into the forms along the sheer.

Figure 5-52. Braces have been installed to support the boat's shape after the removal of the forms.

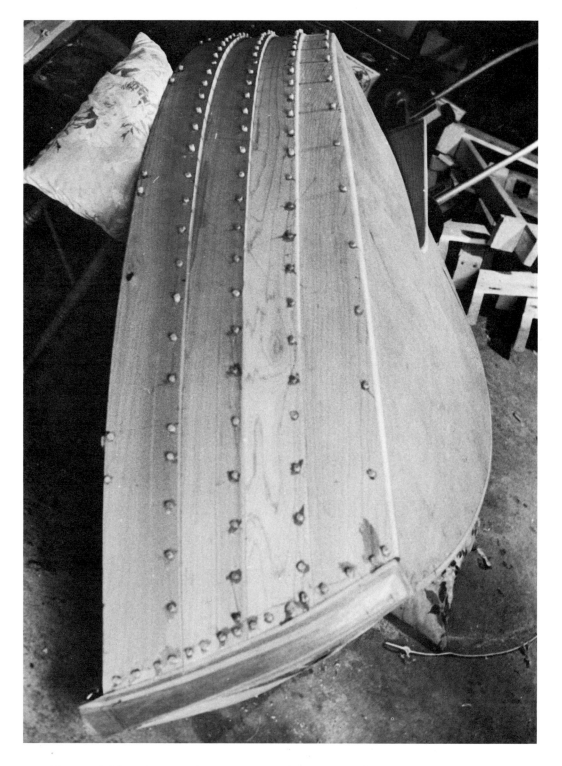

Figure 5-53. The boat has been tipped up so it will be easier to plug the planking rivets.

Chapter 6

COMPLETING
THE INTERIOR

FRAME INSTALLATION

After cutting, shaping, and sanding the frames to the necessary sizes, insert the frames where the forms were (Figure 6-1). Using five screws per frame, attach the frames to the chine from the inside of the boat, and insert screws at each point where the frames meet the planking. Countersink all the screws. After all the frames are installed, the braces may be removed.

Figure 6-1. Braces are used to maintain the boat's shape until the frames are installed in place of the forms.

THE ABC OF BOAT CONSTRUCTION

In the interior, the artistry, beauty, and craftsmanship of boatbuilding come to the fore. This part of the work makes the boat your *own*, not a copy of others made from the same plans. Planking, fitting the stem, and shaping spars, while necessary and beautiful in their own way, are more or less done according to the designer's specifications. The designer still dictates the weight of the woods used for the interior, but, basically, the builder uses his taste and love for high-quality work to determine the finished product. While tillers, daggerboard caps, and seats can be made more simply or easily than the ones shown here, such parts make up the one area in which the boat reflects its builder.

Aside from the aesthetic value, the boat's interior is a good place to try lamination techniques, since the pieces so constructed are always visible and can be checked easily for separations. In the event of a problem, such as a poorly fitting piece, the repair can be accomplished readily. Whereas a separated stem may be quite troublesome, a "topside" problem can be rectified quite easily.

Among the other advantages of lamination are: small pieces may be used, and the resulting piece is often stronger than a similar-size piece of solid wood. Of course, there are some "rules" that must be followed when making any lamination, no matter what the final product.

Generally, laminations must fit precisely, be glued securely, and be finished with pride in fine workmanship. More specifically:

(1) Use pieces that are in proportion to the final size of the finished product.

(2) If you want to accentuate the "laminated look," select light and dark woods for alternating layers.

(3) Place the pieces with the grains running in the same direction. Planing is much easier if the grains match.

(4) Plane the pieces *absolutely flat.* The best tool to use is the long jointer. The job is more difficult if another tool is used.

(5) Make a "dry run" to ensure that all pieces fit properly. When satisfied on this point, mark the pieces in such a way that they are placed together as planned for gluing.

(6) For a strong bond, spread glue on both surfaces, but don't use so much glue that the pieces shift when clamped. There must be enough glue, however, so that some oozes out after clamping.

(7) Clamp the lamination to apply equal pressure along the bond. The usual practice here is to use one clamp every three or four inches (with a small piece of stock inserted to distribute the pressure further).

(8) Let the glue dry thoroughly. This is essential.

(9) Plane, sand, and finish carefully—just as you would treat a solid piece.

With these rules in mind, then, plan laminations for strength and beauty.

LAMINATED GUNWALE

The sheer line may be strengthened in different ways. The designer may call for the use of an inwale (an oak strip attached to the inner edge of each frame), but an attractive alternative is a laminated gunwale (Figures 6-2 through 6-4).

Figure 6-2. Three planed and sanded strips—two mahogany and one cedar—are clamped to the sheer line in a "dry run." The strips are 1/2" thick, 1-1/8" wide, and somewhat shorter than the total length of the boat, in order to allow for installation of breasthook and quarter-knees.

Figure 6-3. The sheer plank serves as a mold for the curve of the gunwale. Clamps must be spaced evenly to ensure even bonding of the glue.

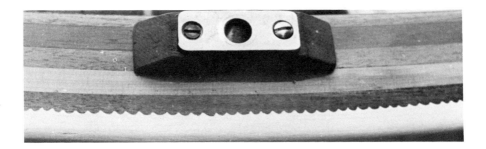

Figure 6-4. A close-up of the finished boat shows the rubrail, the planking, and the alternating shades of the laminated gunwale, topped by the oarlock socket. The gunwale is bedded in Life-Calk and attached by screws from the outside at eight-inch intervals.

RUBRAIL

The rubrail, which is shown completed in Figure 6-4, is made with two pieces of wood—one mahogany and one white oak. They measure ½ inch by ½ inch by the length of the boat. The mahogany piece is placed next to the gunwale, and the oak is placed next to the mahogany. Screw holes are drilled every six inches along the rail. The pieces are screwed temporarily in place and final fitting adjustments are made at stem and transom. After the fit is checked, both rubrail pieces are removed. The mahogany is glued to the oak, and the laminated rail is attached to the sheer plank with Life-Calk. The countersunk screws are then reinserted. After the bedding is thoroughly dry, the rail is shaped and painted.

KNEES

The *Cabin Boy* has three knees and one breasthook: the breasthook at the stem, two quarter-knees at the stern on the sheer, and the transom knee from keelson to transom. Each requires special fitting, which is time-consuming. It is not unusual to spend as much as four or five hours fitting one piece. While they appear rather simple in their placement, the knees have several angles and must fit exactly, so care and patience are required. (Any time after the breasthook is fitted, the laminated stem can be shaped with a wood rasp. It is later finished with several coats of varnish.)

Natural knees cut from apple or white oak trees are the most desirable, since they combine grain and wood strength. Lacking natural knees, a boatbuilder must choose carefully the wood to be used for these vital parts. Wood, under the stress of oar and sail, moves, and this movement must be taken into consideration. Therefore, the grain of the knees must run in a diagonal direction, not across the boat or fore and aft. And the knees must be thick, to discourage splits.

Figure 6-5. The breasthook shaped roughly.

Figure 6-6. The finished breasthook and mast partner in place.

Figure 6-7. One of the quarter-knees shaped to give it a molded appearance.

SEATS

Using white cedar for the seats, trim the whitish sapwood, leaving the wood clear and ready for embellishment. It is a good idea to select the stock carefully so that grains are used to advantage for appearance.

Using the long jointer, plane the edges and surfaces. Since white cedar is one of the easiest woods to plane, it should be smoothed in the workshop. Now make the inlay, as shown in Figures 6-12 through 6-21.

After each inlay is complete, edge each seat (Figure 6-22) and install it (Figure 6-23).

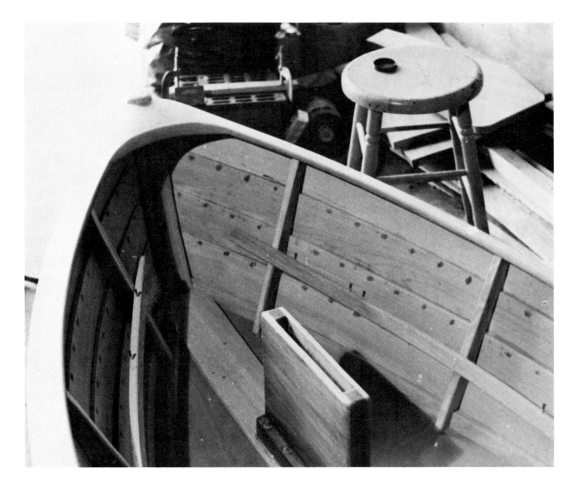

Figure 6-8. Seat risers are screwed into each frame. Seat risers must be installed before the stern knee is installed, since the notch for the seat must be considered when shaping the stern knee.

Figure 6-9. The stern knee is notched for the seat and installed. It is attached from inside the boat, with long screws driven deeply into the keelson and the transom and countersunk.

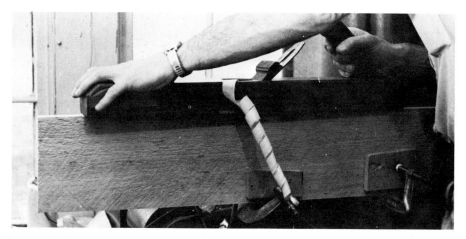

Figure 6-10. Plane the seat edges absolutely flat, using a long jointer.

Figure 6-11. The seat is ready for its inlay.

Figure 6-12. The inlay design is drawn on fairly stiff cardboard.

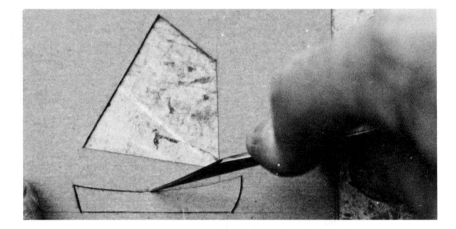

Figure 6-13. The cardboard pattern is cut out, stencil-fashion, with a sharp-edged knife.

Figure 6-14. After the pattern has been cut out, it is traced onto the chosen stock, which should be about 1/8" thick. Furniture inlays are made of much thinner stock, but the weather conditions to which a boat is exposed demand sturdier pieces. Pay particular attention to the grain, which can enhance or detract from the inlay's appearance.

Figure 6-15. The "sail" portion of the inlay has been cut out.

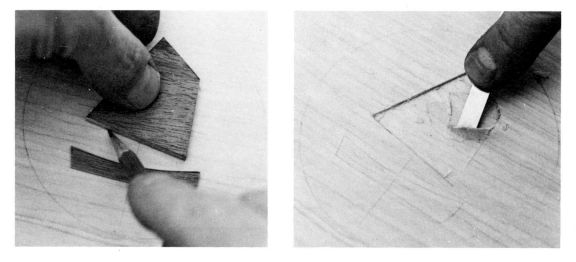

Figure 6-16 (left). After the design elements are cut out with a fine-toothed saw, the edges are sanded, and then the shapes are traced directly onto the seat. Figure 6-17 (right). A chisel is used to gouge the wood from the seat, after the edges have been outlined sharply with a skew. The seat should be cut to a depth slightly less than the 1/8" thickness of the inlay material. The pieces are then glued carefully to prevent water seepage. After the glue is thoroughly dry, the inlay is planed so that it is flush with the seat.

Figure 6-18. The "frame" for the inlaid boat is first drawn as a circle, which is divided into eight equal parts. Then eight separate pieces (each about 1/8" thick) are cut from stock to form an octagon.

Figure 6-19 (left). Each element of the octagonal frame is traced onto the seat to indicate where the wood is to be gouged out. Figure 6-20 (right). The edges of the frame are gouged out with a chisel. These edges, like the central part of the design, are cut slightly less than the 1/8" thickness of the stock. Planing later will make the entire design flush with the seat.

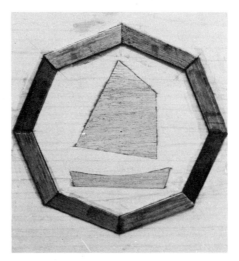

Figure 6-21. The edges of the frame have been glued into position. The next step is planing and sanding for a flush fit. (Note: While it may seem that the glue "bleeding" into the light cedar will detract from the inlay's final appearance, it is not a problem after the wood is varnished. In addition, as it is exposed to the sun, the wood darkens naturally, eliminating what appears here to be a problem.) A single coat of varnish applied at this stage will keep the wood clean while the seat edges are attached.

Figure 6-22. The edge strips are prepared just as for lamination, but they may be glued and screwed onto the seat edges rather than clamped. When the glue is dry, the screws are removed and the holes plugged.

Figure 6-23. The finished seat. Marine bedding compound is used to secure the seat, since it must be removable.

RUDDER

The stock chosen for the rudder of the *Cabin Boy* is Honduras mahogany. While a rudder may seem to be rather mundane, it is possible to make this piece beautiful in shape and in finish, so that it not only performs efficiently and durably, but also is handsome.

The efficiency of the rudder is enhanced by its shape. The leading edge is somewhat thicker than the trailing edge, to avoid disturbing the water too much as it glides on its way. The trailing edge is quite thin, tapered almost to sharpness. The pintles can be attached in the usual way, with the bolts extending through the rudder, but placing the bolts of the upper pintle under the cheekpieces disguises the metal and thus adds to the beauty of the rudder.

The upper pintle is placed on the rudder before the cheekpieces are secured. Its placement is marked and the wood of the cheekpieces is gouged out to receive the pintles and their bolts, so that the cheekpieces will fit flush against the rudder. Before gluing and screwing the cheekpieces in place, it is important to determine the locations for the bolts used to attach the pintle. Bolt the pintle; glue, screw, and plug the cheekpieces; and countersink a hole to the bolt holding the pintle. This hole is plugged by hammering in the wood plug rather than gluing it. Thus, in the event the rudder must be repaired, the plugs and bolts may be removed without trouble. The rudder is attached to the tiller with the pin shown in Figure 6-25.

Figure 6-24 (left). One of the pintles was placed on the rudder before the cheekpieces were secured, thus giving the rudder a sleeker look. Figure 6-25 (right). An oak pin is used to attach the tiller to the rudder. The pin is slightly oval, and the holes in the cheekpieces are also oval, thus allowing the pin to be locked with a slight turn when it is inserted into the rudder.

TILLER

Following the lamination procedures described previously, choose white oak or ash to contrast with mahogany to make the tiller. The total depth of the tiller is about 2½ inches, so that each piece is about ½ inch thick. Other measurements to consider usually are given by the designer.

The hiking stick, barely discernible as most of the bottom lamination layer of the tiller in Figure 6-26, is shown in detail in Figures 6-27 and 6-28. The angle cut on the outboard end of the hiking stick is made so that the stick will not swing out unless the skipper wants it to. It must be put to use by pushing it out to the side.

Figure 6-26. The laminated tiller. The hiking stick is barely visible along the lower edge.

Figure 6-27. A close-up of the tiller, revealing the location of the hiking stick.

Figure 6-28. The underside of the tiller, showing the screw on which the hiking stick pivots.

THE DAGGERBOARD AND ITS CAP

Western red cedar stiffened with white-oak strips on the bottom and the leading edge makes a fine daggerboard. As with the rudder, the leading edge is nearly the thickness of the daggerboard, with the trailing edge tapered substantially.

The laminated cap is made by selecting woods of contrasting shades and cutting them to fit the daggerboard, which is notched for proper fit (Figure 6-30). Figure 6-31 shows that the cap will fit over the daggerboard rather than be glued to the daggerboard itself.

Small, square pieces of mahogany are cut out and used to protect the open grain at the top of the daggerboard (Figure 6-32). The size of each square is equal to the daggerboard thickness. After the wood pieces are glued, and everything is thoroughly dry, sand the cap carefully and attach it to the daggerboard with ordinary bedding compound (Figure 6-33). One screw is countersunk and plugged on one side, two are countersunk and plugged on the other. Do not use glue or a permanent bedding product; daggerboards have been known to need replacing.

Figure 6-29. Oak stiffeners are glued and screwed to the bottom and the leading edge of the daggerboard. It is next shaped to the proper dimensions with a spokeshave.

Figure 6-30. Contrasting shades of wood are clamped and shaped to form the daggerboard cap.

Figure 6-31. The cap fits neatly over the daggerboard.

Figure 6-32. Mahogany squares of alternating patterns are prepared to cover the open grain at the top of the daggerboard. The squares are glued in position.

Figure 6-33. The daggerboard cap is ready for varnishing.

SPARS

The wood usually called for in spar construction is Sitka spruce. Its light weight and natural springiness are legendary among sailboat enthusiasts. Since it must withstand considerable strain for its size, the spar material must be selected with care. Checks often occur in the ends of the pieces of stock. With that in mind, it is best, when ordering, to allow for the trimming of the marred ends. Also, of course, any other markings or defects should be minimal.

After trimming the pieces to the proper lengths, square the lumber to a measurement slightly larger than the finished diameter desired. The initial shaping is done by taking down the corners to make the spar octagonal (Figure 6-34).

The job of shaping and sanding is thus simplified. Care must still be taken, however, to avoid making the spar lopsided. Constant turning of the "stick" will help achieve the desired results. A small piece of cardboard, with the properly sized circumference cut out, is used periodically as a pattern to check progress. As many as three such patterns may be used to check the taper of the spar. After the heel is cut and shaped (Figure 6-35), finish as desired.

Figure 6-34. The finished size of the spar is scribed on the end grain of the stock, and the corners have been taken down to make the spar octagonal.

Figure 6-35. The heel of the spar is cut and shaped as specified by the designer.

OARS

The dimensions of the *Cabin Boy*'s oars are as follows:

> length: 6 feet
> shaft: 1½" in diameter
> blade: 5½" wide, 25" long. The tip is about ⅝" thick.

Using the lamination procedures described earlier, make each oar with three six-foot-long pieces of Sitka spruce and mahogany. Eight 25-inch pieces are added to make the blade.

The *Cabin Boy*'s bronze oarlock sockets are mounted in teak blocks, which are attached to the rail with bolts. A second block under the rail strengthens the upper one.

Figure 6-36. Sitka spruce and mahogany are glued and then clamped every three or four inches. The extra pieces of wood between the clamps help spread the pressure and protect the surfaces.

Figure 6-37. A close-up of the oar blade—after shaping, sanding, and varnishing—reveals no sign of the epoxy.

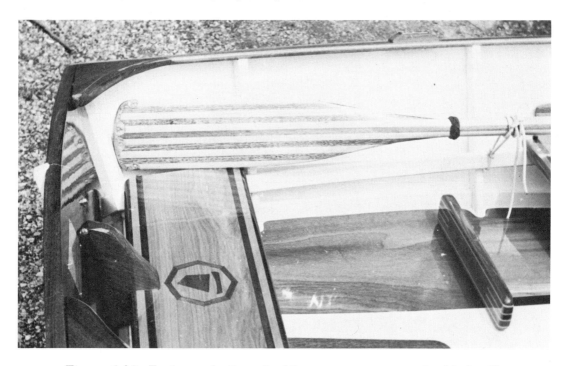

Figure 6-38. Each oar is tipped with copper to protect its blade. The Turk's head encircling the oar shaft keeps water from running along the shaft and into the boat or onto the rower's hands.

Figure 6-39. The Turk's heads and French hitching on either side of the bronze oarlock are decorative, but they also prevent nicks on both rail and oar.

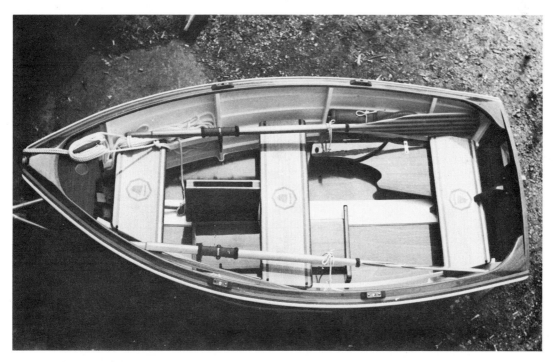

Figure 6-40. The finished skiff, with the oars stowed out of the way yet ready for use.

Chapter 7

WHAT TO PAINT, WHAT TO VARNISH, AND HOW TO DO IT

It is a happy time when you are ready to decide which parts of your boat to paint and which parts to varnish. However, while preparing to do an A-1 job, you may rue the fact that people who will look at your boat probably never will notice the riveting or the way the planks fit "just so." It is a fact of life that what will be noticed is the last coat of varnish or paint.

Every boatowner has his own opinion about the "proper" finishing of a boat. It is not uncommon to see yellow, pink, or lavender paint on boats. Some are in agreement with Henry Ford and his Model T: black is best. Small boats seem to have remained a more-or-less-consistent white.

The first decision involves the amount of varnish to be used. After paint is on new wood, there is no changing one's mind. Although varnish nowadays seems to evoke distaste at worst and ambivalence at best, consider the common reaction in the past to a boat finished with varnish: "She's beautiful!" There can be no argument with that statement. Besides preserving the wood, varnish provides a luster that cannot be duplicated in any other finish. Tales of its preservation powers have even been told by divers recovering wrecks from the Mediterranean; while metal rusted and paints peeled, the fine, oil-based varnish was reported to be nearly perfect.

"It's too much work." In this statement, ambivalence is exposed. While admiring the qualities of varnish, the modern boatman would rather have the upkeep handled by someone else. This attitude is no doubt encouraged by plastic-and-teak-trim-boat salesmen, and it is a disservice to the art of finishing practices. Look over a boatyard sometime. Don't the plastic boats need cleaning and/or painting? Don't the wooden boats with painted surfaces need attention? Naturally any boat needs to be worked on to look its best. Only someone victimized by Madison Avenue would say, "She doesn't need any upkeep." Henry David Thoreau made the point years ago, when he said something like, "You don't own things; they own you." Assuming, then, that you have chosen to be owned by a boat, face up to that responsibility. The next choice is not between upkeep and no upkeep; it is between one kind of upkeep and another kind of upkeep.

"It's too fussy." Granted that the original finishing job may be rather detailed, the year-after-year maintenance is less than that required for fiberglass boats. Keeping a plastic dinghy in tiptop shape requires cleaning, polishing, and usually painting. Compare that with a light sanding job and one coat of varnish. Besides, the varnish work is aesthetically rewarding: how much more pleasant to see your labor result in that satiny finish! Incidentally, over the years I have noticed that people tend to treat a boat with more respect when it is varnished: a plastic boat may invite misuse, but a beautifully finished piece of cedar may invite care.

All laminations and inlays should be varnished to enhance their beauty. Oak is hard to varnish, so it is best to paint anything made with oak. Paint can also be used for contrast with the varnished brightwork.

Now, assuming that you have decided what to paint and what to varnish, on with the finishing.

If you decide on the same scheme of finishing as that pictured here (Figures 7-1 and 7-2), the following supplies will be needed:

1 quart varnish (spar varnish with ultraviolet-filter additive)
1 small, natural-bristle, 1½"-wide brush, tapered and straight-cut
2 tack rags
sandpaper: coarse, medium, fine, and extra-fine
1 gallon turpentine
1 package 8-ounce plastic tumblers
cheesecloth or nylon stockings
1 quart high-gloss white yacht paint
1 quart white undercoat paint

The order of the work is as follows:
(1) sand and clean new wood surfaces of the boat
(2) prepare brush

Figure 7-1. The Cabin Boy *completed. The varnished sheer plank provides freeboard contrast, just as the white-painted rubrail provides contrast between the varnished plank and the laminated gunwale. (Painting rather than varnishing the rubrail is wise, because it is likely to be bumped frequently.)*

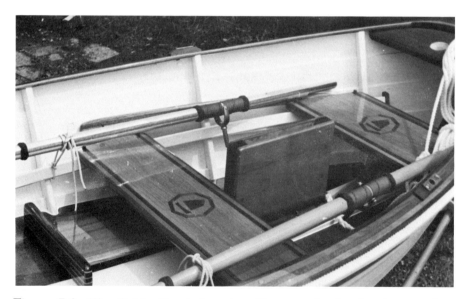

Figure 7-2. The Cabin Boy's *interior. Because the laminations and inlays are not painted, the inside is painted white to contrast with the darker gloss of the varnish. The keelson, being painted white, invites passengers to "step to the center" of the dinghy. The teak mast partner is left unfinished, partly because of its oil content and partly because the mast is taken out and inserted frequently. Leaving it "plain" prevents chips or mars.*

(3) prepare varnish (By varnishing first, paint spills, which are nearly impossible to remove from bare wood, will be avoided.)
(4) sand and clean between coats of varnish
(5) paint with undercoat (thinned, then full strength)
(6) paint with high-gloss white

SANDING

Prepare the wood by hand sanding it thoroughly. Power sanding leaves marks that cannot be disguised by the finishing materials. On all woods except the very soft, such as spruce or cedar, start with coarse sandpaper. Next use medium, then fine, then extra-fine (220). Each time a new type is used, be sure to sand well enough to remove the sanding marks left by the coarser paper. Always sand *with* the grain in evenly pressured strokes. Patience is a virtue well rewarded in this activity. After sanding, the removal of the dust is most important, and it is best to take the boat to a clean area. Lacking that convenience, sweep the floor and allow a 24-hour settling period. Just before application, use a tack rag to remove any remaining particles. After each coat of varnish or paint, sand the surface lightly to dull it and promote adhesion of the new coat. Changing the extra-fine sandpaper each time it becomes clogged with the finishing product seems extravagant, but rubbing in the bits of varnish or paint is a disaster. After each light sanding, the surface must be tack-ragged. After three or four coats of varnish, if you wish to wash off the accumulated dust, be sure to dry the surface with a chamois. Never varnish on a damp surface.

PREPARING THE BRUSH

As specified, a natural-bristle brush is desirable for both varnishing and painting. This brush need not be expensive. In fact, it may be advantageous to use a cheap brush until a satisfactory technique is developed. Regardless of your choice, wash the brush in warm, sudsy water and rinse it thoroughly before use. This rids it of dust and loose hairs, which can cause trouble during application. Wrap the damp brush in a paper towel to retain its shape.

Just before using, dip the brush in turpentine to cut any soap that may have been left in the brush. (After use, the brush is cleaned in *warm* turpentine: pour the turpentine into a small jar, place the jar in a pan of water, and slowly heat it.) This process keeps flecks of varnish or paint from hardening in the "innards" of the brush. Keep changing the turpentine until it remains clear after the brush is placed in the jar. Follow this procedure with the warm-water wash and rinse. Wrap the damp brush in a paper towel until its next use.

VARNISHING

While many companies tout their product as superior to others because of some mysterious agent, I have found that most brands of spar varnish are acceptable. The one "secret ingredient" that may indeed be advantageous is the ultraviolet-filter additive. I have had experience with "plain" and ultraviolet types and have found that there definitely seems to be a more lasting gloss in the filtered products. Many name brands offer this additive. Again, I prefer the oil-based "true" varnishes to the urethane finishing products. While the plastic types are similar in application, they do not seem to hold up as well as the oil varnishes. After one season's use on a six-coat finish, I have seen noticeable wear on places where lines met the surface. Also, I have used various brands, one on top of the other, apparently without detriment. I have not mixed oil- and plastic-based products, though, and I do not recommend such a practice.

The ideal weather for varnishing is a temperature of around 70 degrees with a low moisture content in the atmosphere. Try to find an insect-free area in which to apply varnish. Even though modern products have agents that speed the drying process, a temperature much colder than 70 degrees invites a thickened, slow-drying, difficult-to-work-with varnish. Of course, reading directions carefully and following the manufacturer's instructions are always good practices. One general suggestion: always stir a can of varnish; never shake it, or you will find it is full of bubbles.

After the can is opened, punch small holes in the rim. This allows drips to return to the can, avoiding waste. For the application of both paint and varnish, I recommend eight-ounce-capacity plastic tumblers. They are easy to handle while you move about the boat, and they can be discarded rather than cleaned. For painting, one tumbler at a time is sufficient, but for varnishing, two will be needed. Strain the varnish into one of the tumblers. Fill it about halfway. Let it settle while you prepare the brush. Dip the brush into the varnish about halfway. Quickly move the brush to the second tumbler and let the excess varnish drip into it. (Squeezing the brush against the edge of the tumbler will cause air bubbles to form in the varnish in the brush.)

Finally, start spreading the varnish. Try to cover about one square foot at a time. Develop a technique that covers, yet leaves no brush marks. Too much varnish will run, too little will create small bubbles on the surface. Again, aim for the "just-right" stroke.

Although the original task of varnishing requires time and effort, the yearly or biyearly upkeep is minimal after that. The purpose is to protect the wood. Weathering can occur only if water is allowed to penetrate the surface and settle under the varnish. To avoid this, six or seven base coats are necessary. Figure 7-3 shows a quarter-knee with two coats of varnish. While it would be considered shiny and passable to some, it is obviously less acceptable than the mirrorlike finish of the work in Figure 7-4. While a nick could penetrate to the wood in Figure 7-3, the many coats in Figure 7-4 provide a substantial barrier. Stopping at two coats invites an annual stripping, sanding, and varnishing job to maintain a high-quality look for your boat and to ensure protection for the wood. If, on the other hand, six or seven coats are applied originally, the maintenance is reduced to a light sanding and replacement of the sanded-off coat of varnish.

I find the fall to be a more appropriate time to varnish than the spring. Indian summer provides the drier air and insect-free days necessary for the fine work. Also, when the first warm days of spring arrive, I am ready to take advantage of them. The choice is clear: two coats and refinish annually, or six to eight coats and minimal year-to-year maintenance.

(As an aside, I would like to relate a personal experience regarding my 12-foot gaff-rigged sloop. I applied a six- or seven-coat base of varnish to some parts of the boat. After one season, the grain of the wood seemed to rise beneath the varnish. Rather than sand and refinish, I sanded lightly with extra-fine paper and added two coats of varnish. The next season I added two more coats. After the second season the grain seemed to "settle," and now the wood is smooth. I recommend this gradual building-up of a glossy surface.)

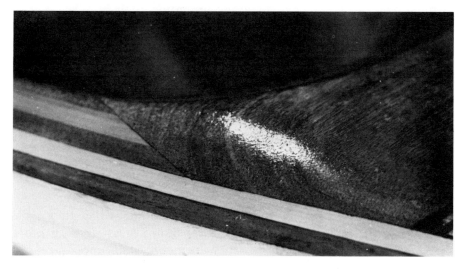

Figure 7-3. A quarter-knee with two coats of varnish.

Figure 7-4. A quarter-knee with multiple coats of varnish, producing a perfect mirror image.

PAINTING

After doing the brightwork, the painting is very rewarding. That shine of the varnish is contrasted with the white, and the sight is a pleasure!

Before beginning, prepare the brush as mentioned earlier. Apply an undercoat of white thinned with turpentine to help fill the grain of the wood. The second undercoat application should be full strength, followed by two coats of high-gloss white. Sand lightly after each application. Paint buildup is not advantageous, since modern materials cover quite well and the wood will be protected sufficiently with four coats of paint. When repainting during later maintenance, sand lightly and replace the paint with a light touch.

MAINTAINING THE FINISH

Be sure to protect the boat before, during, and after use. Weathering and rot are easily avoided, but difficult to handle when they have taken hold. Never has the "ounce of prevention" saying been more true than around a boat. The four elements that encourage the growth of mold, mildew, and, finally, rot are warmth, dampness, darkness, and dirt. Store the boat in such a way as to avoid all four.

A lightweight dinghy is easily stored upside-down, but air circulation must be assured. A small rack that keeps the boat off damp grass or dirt is easy to make. It can be as simple as two boards under stem and stern or as elaborate as the kitchen table. (A larger skiff should be provided with a rack and should be covered with canvas when not in use. The cover should allow free air circulation.)

As with fine silver, the best way to care for boats is to use them. The sun destroys the spores of mold and mildew during sailing, but afterward, a five-minute wash and wipe with a soft towel should be a routine part of the sailing experience. Also, when washing and drying the boat, you become aware of rigging that needs attention, or nicks that need filling with varnish. To just sail and then drag the boat to the nearest shore and leave it "abandoned" is to miss one of the special qualities of sailing. When care is taken to build a fine craft, how rewarding it is to keep it shining and fresh-looking.

Chapter 8

THE FINAL TOUCHES

Some gear and fittings that reflect the craftsman's personality (and enthusiasm) are all that remain to be made once the finished craft has been hoisted onto its trailer. There is, for example, the boathook, retriever of lost treasures and lifesaver at dockside. Cleats, blocks, belaying pin, and sail stop—all made of wood—contribute that extra touch of craftsmanship. A bilge pump, a welcome and efficient substitute for the cut-off Clorox container, completes the *Cabin Boy*'s sailing paraphernalia.

LAMINATED BOATHOOK

A boathook is an excellent test of laminating skill. While the joiner work still has to be of the highest quality, the hook is evaluated easily, and any mistake can be remedied. If success is achieved in this lamination, then it is possible to be more confident in making other items with the same procedure. The general rules of lamination (see Chapter 6) must be followed for the boathook: angles must be well matched and cut; surfaces must be planed absolutely true and flat; and the gluing and clamping must exert equal pressure along the entire hook to bend evenly.

The taste of the builder is reflected in the pattern of the woods chosen for both shaft and hook parts. The materials for the boathook (Figure 8-6) were not chosen haphazardly. While a hook made of Sitka spruce alone might lack the strength necessary for its job, the combination with mahogany makes it worthy of its task. On the other hand, the weight of the mahogany is lessened by combining it with the spruce. Together, the light weight of the spruce and the strength of the mahogany make a beautiful, useful boathook.

The materials listed below are for duplication of the lamination pattern illustrated. Make the proper adjustments if a different pattern of woods is used.

MATERIALS

Shaft

three pieces Sitka spruce, $\frac{3}{8}$″ x $1\frac{5}{8}$″ x 4′
two pieces mahogany, $\frac{3}{8}$″ x $1\frac{5}{8}$″ x 4′

Hook

three pieces mahogany, $\frac{1}{4}$″ x $1\frac{1}{2}$″ x $5\frac{1}{4}$″
two pieces Sitka spruce, $\frac{1}{4}$″ x $1\frac{1}{2}$″ x $5\frac{1}{4}$″
epoxy glue: 4-ounce tubes of parts A and B
leather strips to protect hook points during use

The boathook should be stowed to allow for easy access. It is surprising how quickly it may have to be available for use, especially if the boat is being sailed singlehanded.

Figure 8-1. Three Sitka spruce strips alternate with two mahogany strips to form the shaft of the boathook.

Figure 8-2. Shaft and hook sections are clamped together. Note that the contrasting shades of the shaft are reversed for the hook. After the desired general shape is fitted and planed, the sections are glued liberally and then clamped every three inches.

Figure 8-3. The hook's outline is marked on the glued pieces, and the final shaping can proceed.

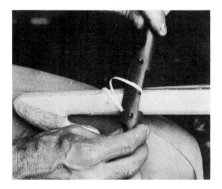

Figure 8-4. The spokeshave, used almost like a sculptor's tool, shapes the laminated wood gradually. When the boathook is ready for finishing, it should be varnished and revarnished until 6 or 7 coats have been applied. Medium, then fine, and finally extra-fine (220) sandpaper should be used between coats.

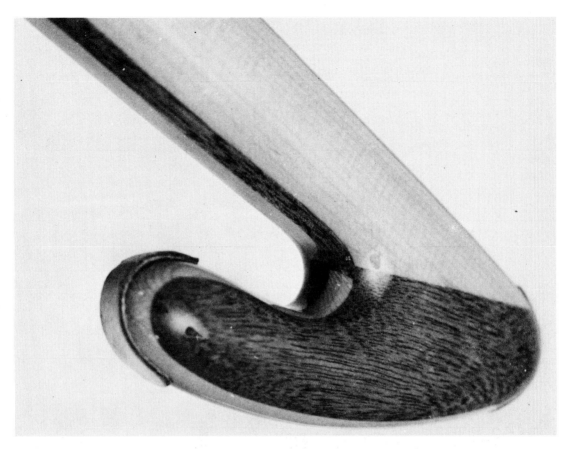

Figure 8-5. A close-up of the boathook, showing the small leather strips attached to both points to keep the hook from damaging any surface it may hit. The leather also protects the hook itself.

Figure 8-6. The completed boathook.

SILENT WONDERS: CLEATS, BELAYING PIN, SAIL STOP

Sails and the lines that control them can be the greatest of enemies as well as the greatest of friends to the sailor. Properly raised and secured, with halyards and sheets tended properly, the sails do your bidding. Properly lowered and secured, they will remain under control and their lives will be extended noticeably. The key word is *secured*. Whether you use cleats or pins for belaying lines is a matter of choice.

Belaying a main sheet for quick release and a halyard for security are skills to be learned by skipper and crew alike. Handling a sail, especially while it's being lowered, is another tricky but solvable problem. I once heard a sailor say, when it came to lowering the sail, that he wished man had retained a prehensile tail. To him it just seemed impossible at times to manage the rudder, sheet, halyard, *and* the sail, all at the same time.

The cleats, belaying pin, and sail stop included here as "silent wonders" may simplify somewhat the usual line-handling and sail-handling procedures.

MOORING AND JAM CLEATS

Cleats are commonplace and utilitarian. That may be one reason why they are often overlooked. Wooden cleats are especially beneficial for the small-boat sailor. First of all, they are attractive; second, their type of upkeep can be preselected by the owner; third, they are a bargain; and, not to be discounted, their design is unique and serviceable.

A varnished deck may "need" a contrasting, painted cleat to highlight its beauty. A painted deck, on the other hand, may look best with an easy-to-care-for, oiled lignum-vitae cleat. A locust cleat, varnished to show its beautiful and unusual grain, may be yet another choice. It should be remembered that teak, so useful for many small-boat items, is not the best choice for a cleat, because its strength is less than that of oak or other hardwoods. The bargain price is hard to beat. A homemade wooden cleat will be much less expensive than a purchased one, especially if it is made from scrap wood.

When cutting and shaping the cleat you have in mind, make adjustments to fit your needs, but do not change the basic design.

Wooden cleats (Figures 8-7 through 8-12) are a handsome addition to any boat.

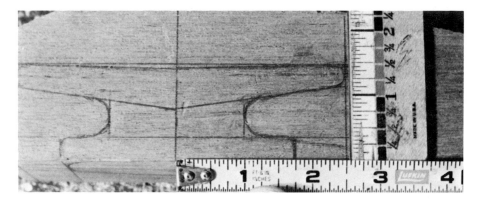

Figure 8-7. The desired shape of the mooring cleat is drawn on the wood, which should be slightly larger than the finished size (in this case, 5" long, 1-1/2" high, and 7/8" thick at the top).

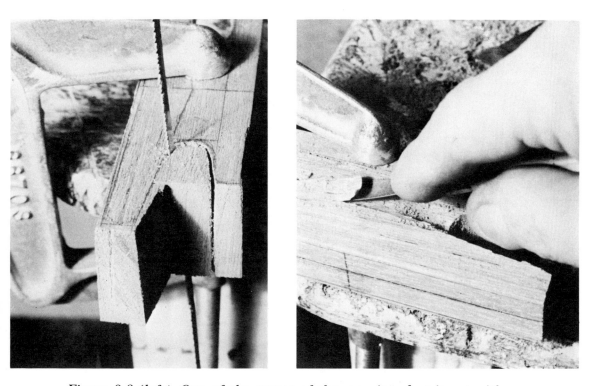

Figure 8-8 (left). One of the curves of the mooring cleat is cut with a bow saw fitted with a 1/8" fine-toothed blade. Figure 8-9 (right). A carver's gouge is used with a light touch to cut away just enough wood to retain the strength of the wide wooden base yet provide for the smooth running of the line.

Figure 8-10. A rattail file is used to smooth the cleat to its final shape. The cleat then is sanded and holes are drilled for bolts.

Figure 8-11. The finished mooring cleat. Every edge is rounded, allowing free movement of the lines. Snagging of sails and other gear is kept to a minimum. The wide base is elevated slightly so the line does not wear or rub the mast partner (where the cleat is mounted) excessively. The two holes provide for the bolts that go through cleat, mast partner, and a supporting block underneath that ensures firm anchoring.

Figure 8-12. A jam cleat made according to the same technique as the mooring cleat. The space in which the line is jammed is not chosen haphazardly: it is made to receive a particular size of line.

BELAYING PIN

While the design of the belaying pin is simpler than that of the cleat, two of the cleat's features must be retained in the pin: all edges must be rounded, and a wide base (shaft) is needed for strength.

The method of construction (drawing, cutting, shaping) remains basically the same as for the cleats. Before drawing the outline of the pin on the wood, however, it is best to draw a cardboard pattern so that any subsequent pins will be the same size. As with the cleats, lignum vitae is the first choice, although white oak and locust are good substitutes.

Figure 8-13. The shaft of the belaying pin has been cut out, and the center line has been redrawn on it. A cardboard pattern was used to trace the design on the wood.

Figure 8-14. The top portion of the belaying pin has been squared and then filed gradually. The eventual round shape of the top is achieved with a rasp and a file and sanding.

Figure 8-15. The completed belaying pin, which is 7-1/2" long. Its shaft is 1/2" in diameter and its "collar" is 1-1/8" in diameter.

SAIL STOP

This design, originated by the author, deserves some special consideration. No matter how artistic it is, no design is worthwhile unless it performs its ordained task, which in this case is to secure the furled sail quickly, efficiently, and safely.

In a very small boat, it is desirable to furl the sail quickly once it has been lowered, for space in the boat is at a premium, and time may be also, if landing at a dock or picking up a mooring. What is needed is a sail stop that can be secured quickly. While a piece of shock cord with a metal hook is often used for this purpose, it has some shortcomings, and a comparison with the wooden version may be warranted.

SHOCK CORD WITH METAL HOOK	WOODEN SAIL STOP
Metal hooks mean possible damage to boat, sail, and/or crew member.	The wooden stop is rounded on all surfaces.
A certain size must be ordered, thus limiting versatility.	Since knots or loops are not a permanent part of the construction, versatility is not lost.
Shock cord stretches, then "pinches."	Nylon line is adjustable to the size of sail. Comfortable fit is gained without excess pinching of sail or rubbing on the boom.
Two hands are needed to release the hook, because it must be controlled to avoid hitting boat or crew member.	Built-in jam cleat can be released easily and safely with one hand.
Original cost is high.	Minimal cost involved.
Stowage is a problem. If it is not banging or scratching, it is corroding.	Stowage is no problem.

To make the sail stop shown here (Figures 8-16 and 8-17), you will need a piece of wood ½ inch by one inch by 2⅞ inches. (If you use white oak, it should be painted. Lignum vitae or teak may be oiled. Maple is an interesting alternative.) The line used is nylon, ³⁄₁₆ inch to ¼ inch, about four feet long.

Figure 8-16. The sail stop has been cut out roughly. The slots have been cut first with a dovetail saw. The hole on the right, for the eye splice, has been drilled on the center line with a 3/8" bit; it handles a 1/4" line. The right-hand slot, drilled below the center line with a 1/4" bit, allows the line to run easily. The left-hand slot, which jams the line, has been drilled with a 1/8" bit. The left-hand slot is not rounded on its inner edge: the edge must be kept straight and the slot narrow so that the line will pull itself tighter with natural pressure.

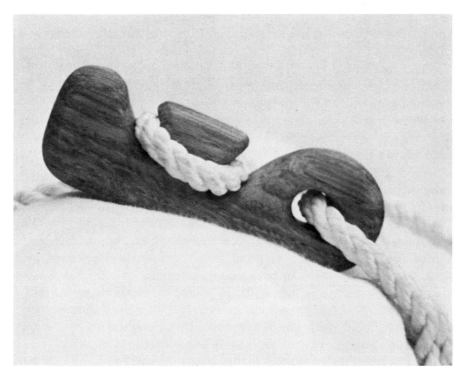

Figure 8-17. The completed sail stop. The jammed line in the left-hand slot will not release until it has been pulled from the right-hand slot. The line renders through the larger, right-hand slot for tightening, and jams in the smaller, left-hand slot.

WOODEN BLOCKS? WOODEN BLOCKS!

The search for the "newest" and "most improved" blocks drives many yachtsmen to marine stores and catalogs year after year. Their idea seems to be to match the most modern boat and sails with the most modern blocks. Salesmen and ads are quick to point out the most-desired qualities: durability, easy maintenance, and efficiency. What is usually ignored is the cost, but modern research must somehow be subsidized. This practice is indeed a shame when you reason along with Hervey Garrett Smith in his *Arts of the Sailor*: "For upwards of five hundred years ships were fitted with rope-strapped blocks. . . . If they were so obviously practical through all those centuries why shouldn't they be equally useful today?" Mr. Smith discovered, or should we say rediscovered, the outstanding features of wooden blocks that are available to today's sailor.

The durability of any block is dependent on its material *and* its method of construction. Modern glues combine with unsurpassable woods like teak or lignum vitae to form the most durable blocks you can have.

The cost of wooden blocks is embarrassingly low. Any boatbuilder should be able to supply his boat with all the blocks he needs by scrounging carefully through the scrap box.

While teak blocks demand an occasional oiling, rope-stropping acts as a cushion against knocks, eliminating unsightly scratches. The wise sailor knows that no material is "maintenance-free." Everything has to be wiped and cleaned and polished if it is to work and look well. The chore seems easier when the block being maintained is a beautiful one, handmade with pride.

The efficiency of blocks custom-designed for your boat cannot be duplicated by any mass-produced item available in a marine store. A rope-stropped block can be a tail block or a jib sheet pendant, or a block with a becket. It can have double strapping or a double sheave. It can do any necessary job with only simple variations of the basic construction. Efficiency adds to its beauty. Seeing a fitting perform the way it should, with line flowing silently through clatterless wood, is a pleasing complement to the sailing experience.

The seeming incongruities of the scientific and the simple, and of the ancient and the modern, can be turned to advantage by the boat-man with enough imagination and persistence to create for himself the fittings that make his boat *his* boat.

Once you have decided to make your own wooden blocks, the first step is to acquire the sheaves, preferably by making them, since a block usually is made to fit its sheave precisely. The size of the sheave is determined by the size of the line. I chose $3/8$-inch line because of its handling ease, although $5/16$-inch line would also work with the sheave described below.

MAKING A SHEAVE

Taking care and using logical techniques can take some of the difficulty out of constructing a *round* object that must turn evenly on an axle.

Three steps complete the shaping of the circle:

(1) Mark the circle well. The circle for the sheave should be scribed precisely and visibly. It is your guide to a round shape and must be clear throughout the process.

(2) Trim closely, squaring the circle first. Trimming the circle close to the outline, but allowing some room for final shaping, is important (Figure 8-18). The old adage about tackling a job by breaking it down into manageable steps is operative here. Squaring and then cutting corners to make an octagon (Figure 8-19) is generally easier than trying to force a saw around a circular course.

(3) Shape the sheave evenly with a rasp. The final shaping should be done with a light hand. The rasp will make an elliptical rather than round shape if you fail to keep the outline visible.

The drilling of the sheave hole is extremely important. The line will run smoothly through the finished block only if the hole is centered exactly. After using a ⅜-inch bit, try to insert the brass pin for the block. It should fit very snugly. Then it should be enlarged very carefully with a rattail file. Washers will be placed in a recessed portion of the sheave (see Figure 8-23) cut around the hole with a carver's gouge and "dug out" with a bent chisel. The finished sheave appears in Figure 8-20.

Figure 8-18. After the circle is scribed for the sheave, it is "squared" with a hardback saw. The hole in the center must be large enough so that it can be used later as a guide for drilling the hole for the pin.

Figure 8-19. An octagon is formed from the square. Final shaping of the circle is done with a rasp.

BLOCK CONSTRUCTION

Included here are two common, simple blocks. The metal-strapped block is made in four separate pieces and glued securely. The other, a solid block, is rope-stropped. These blocks are basic and can be changed to fit particular requirements. The stainless-steel strap adds strength without much weight, and the rope-stropped block is especially useful as a tail block and is extremely adaptable. Both are very light and require little in the way of upkeep.

STEEL-STRAPPED BLOCK

The materials needed to make a steel-strapped block are as follows:

Wood

hardwoods: lignum vitae, teak, cherry, white oak, maple, walnut
$\frac{3}{8}''$ x $1\frac{5}{8}''$ x $3\frac{1}{2}''$, two pieces for cheeks
$\frac{13}{16}''$ x $1\frac{5}{8}''$ x $1\frac{1}{8}''$, two pieces for separators

Metal

stainless-steel strap, $\frac{1}{16}''$ x $1''$ x $12''$
$\frac{3}{8}''$ brass rod for pin
two brass washers

Glue

epoxy: 4-ounce tubes, parts A and B

Sheave

$\frac{9}{16}''$ x $1\frac{1}{4}''$ diameter with $\frac{3}{8}''$ drilled hole (a roller-bearing type is best, a plastic one will do, and directions for making a wooden one have already been given)

Begin construction of the steel-strapped block by shaping the separators of the block to fit around the circumference of the sheave. Next, bend the stainless-steel strap and, with a hacksaw, make a cut on each side of the bend to taper the "eye" of the block. Not too much steel should be removed, because the strength of the finished block depends largely on this metal strap. Shape the recess for the strap in the wooden separators. This recess is $\frac{1}{16}$ inch, exactly the same as the metal's thickness (Figure 8-20).

Assemble the separators, strap, and sheave (Figure 8-21). Be sure that everything fits well and that there is at least $\frac{1}{8}$ inch clearance for sheave and line to move freely. Add the cheekpieces. Before clamping the pieces to be glued, insert cushions of scrap wood. They will prevent marring of the finished surfaces. In addition, these cushions ensure even pressure, so important for the strength of the bond. Apply glue freely, clamp securely, and allow to dry thoroughly (Figures 8-23 and 8-24).

Following the same procedure used to make the sheave, trim off the steel straps and the wooden cheeks. Using a rasp and a file, shape them gradually. Take special note of the lower portion of the block. Using a rattail file, make the groove for the line deeper than that in the sheave. That way, the line will roll on the sheave without rubbing on the block, which would cause unnecessary wear (Figure 8-25).

The hole that receives the pin should be drilled through one cheekpiece and through both straps (Figure 8-26). Place washers in the recesses in the sheave and "thread" the sheave onto the pin. Lightly glue a wooden plug into place, so that the pin can be taken out and the sheave replaced if necessary. If additional strength is needed, or if you lack confidence in the gluing job, rivets may be inserted through the block to fasten together cheeks, straps, and separators.

Oiling is especially recommended for the block. Teak and lignum vitae have natural oils that glorify the grain of the wood, but application of additional oil will ensure the continuance of this rich look. Boiled linseed oil is recommended. The finished block appears in Figure 8-27.

Figure 8-20. The components of the steel-strapped block. From left: two cheekpieces, sheave and two separators, and stainless-steel strap.

Figure 8-21. The separators, sheave, and strap are positioned for fit.

Figure 8-22. An end-on view of the block shows clearly the recesses that have been cut in the lower separator to receive the steel strap.

Figure 8-23. All parts of the steel-strapped block are glued and clamped. Two pieces of scrap wood protect the block during clamping.

Figure 8-24. The block must be allowed to dry thoroughly before it is trimmed, shaped, and finished.

Figure 8-25. The block has been trimmed roughly and then shaped more precisely with a rasp and a file.

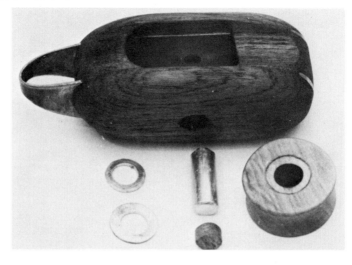

Figure 8-26. Elements of the steel-strapped block before final assembly. Included are: two brass washers, a brass pin, a sheave, and a plug.

Figure 8-27. The steel-strapped block, complete.

ROPE–STROPPED TAIL BLOCK

The materials needed for a rope-stropped tail block are as follows:

Wood

hardwoods, as for the steel-strapped block (this particular block is made of air-dried black maple)
one piece, 1½″ x 1½″ x 3⅜″

Rope

5⁄16″ or ⅜″, seven feet or more

Metal

⅜" rod for pin
two washers

Sheave

⁹⁄₁₆" x 1¼" diameter with ⅜" drilled hole (a roller-bearing sheave is best, a plastic one will do, and instructions for making a wooden one have been given).

The rope-stropped block is made according to the steps illustrated in Figures 8-28 through 8-34. Oiling is recommended as a practical finish for the rope-stropped block, just as with the metal-strapped block.

Figure 8-28. The sheave placement is marked off on the penciled-in outline of the tail block.

Figure 8-29. Squaring the block eliminates unnecessary hand work during the final shaping.

Figure 8-30. One-eighth-inch holes are drilled in the sheave opening as a first step toward removal of the wood. The hole for the pin has been drilled through both cheeks, since this block is a solid piece of wood, and the line is adequate to keep the pin in place.

Figure 8-31. A chisel is used to gouge out the sheave opening. Further shaping of the opening is done with a curved riffler and then a round riffler. The shell of the block is then shaped gradually with a plane.

Figure 8-32. The groove that holds the line in place is made with a rattail file. The depth of the groove should be equal to about one-half the diameter of the line to be used: the groove should be deep enough to hold the rope, but it should not be so deep as to weaken the shell.

Figure 8-33. The block is ready for assembly. Shown are: the pin, two washers, sheave, shell.

Figure 8-34. The finished tail block, complete with 5/16" strop. The eye splice should be so tight that you would think no seizing would be necessary. However, seizing should still be done to prevent raveling; 1/8" nylon line was used here.

A GOOD-LOOKING—AND EFFICIENT—PUMP

It may be next to impossible to find a boat owner who regards his bilge pump as one of the more beautiful pieces of gear in his boat; a bilge pump is supposed to be utilitarian—no more, no less. But this need not be the case. The pump shown here is small enough to stow easily (it is 14½ inches high), efficient (it pumps six gallons a minute), and attractive (it is made with beautiful woods and brass).

Using this pump is no problem, since the shaft is short and the base has an adequate foothold. Instead of holding the pump awkwardly with one hand and pumping with the other, you can use both hands on the handle, making your stroke more efficient.

Practically speaking, wood is a good material for a bilge pump; the elements can be repaired easily. No longer must you be at the mercy of the sales clerk who states simply, "It can't be fixed; you're better off just buying a new one."

An added feature of wood is its potential for personalization. For the boatman who so desires, an initial, a silhouette of his boat, or some other design can be added with inlays or carvings.

This pump, made in your shop during the off season, can pay off in both increased efficiency and beauty: an object of admiration and pride.

MATERIALS

Below are the materials needed to make a wooden bilge pump:

Wood

pump barrel: teak, white cedar, or red cedar
    ¾" x 3½" x 12", two pieces
    ¾" x 2" x 12", two pieces
cap: teak only
    1¼" x 4" x 4", one piece
base: teak only
    1¼" x 4" x 6", one piece
hose clamp: teak only
    1¾" x 4" x 4", one piece

Brass

2 feet of ⅜" or ½"
1 foot of ¼"
1 foot of ⅛"

Screws

20 ¾" flathead no. 8 (pump barrel)
10 2" flathead no. 8 (cap, base, hose clamp)
 2 1½" flathead no. 8 (hose clamp)
 3 ⅜" flathead (leather intake valve)

Leather

⅛″ thick by 6″ square (intake and exhaust valves)

Hose

1½″ diameter by at least 2′ 8″ long

Glue

epoxy: 4-ounce size, parts A and B

Bedding Compound

one pint

MAKING THE BARREL

The measurements specified for the pump barrel are the *finished* measurements, so start with four slightly larger pieces of wood. (Teak takes fastenings well, it resists rot, and it's less subject to expansion and contraction than other woods. Red cedar, however, is a suitable substitute that will give many years of worthy service.) Plane and sand just enough to square the edges and make them smooth. Adjust the iron in your plane until a uniform shaving is achieved: it should be one thin shaving the same width as the wood you are planing (Figure 8-35).

When the four pieces measure the 2 inch and 3½ inch widths specified, cut two rabbets in each of the two wider pieces (Figure 8-36). While this step can be omitted, it simplifies clamping and drilling. The rabbet plane, with its razor-sharp blade, cuts smoothly enough so that sanding is not needed.

After the four pieces are fitted together (Figure 8-37), they can be drilled. After drilling the holes 2½ inches apart (measured from center to center), screw all the pieces together to make sure all edges line up properly. Use 10 ¾-inch screws on each of the wider sides.

Mark the edges of the barrel so that when gluing you won't have to guess which piece fits where. Mix glue, apply to lengthwise edges, and screw the sides into place. Allow thorough drying, after which the screws may be removed and the holes plugged. (I use a contrasting wood for plugs, but it's a matter of preference.) Trim and sand the plugs (Figure 8-38).

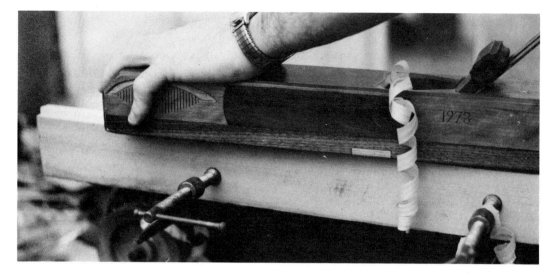

Figure 8-35. When the edges of the bilge pump barrel are planed with a long jointer, the shavings must be uniform.

Figure 8-36. The bilge pump barrel's four main elements, two of which are rabbeted for a tight fit.

Figure 8-37. The four pieces of the pump barrel are ready to be drilled.

Figure 8-38. The pump barrel, after being glued, screwed, plugged, trimmed, and sanded.

MAKING CAP AND BASE

The cap of the pump is a simple square with beveled edges; the base is larger than the cap (Figure 8-39). The base extensions form the footrest for pumping. The underside of the base is recessed so that the water will flow freely into the pump (Figure 8-40).

With a $^{15}\!/_{64}$ -inch bit, drill four rows of five holes each in the base, and then enlarge the holes to make slots by connecting adjacent pairs of holes (Figure 8-42). Smooth the edges of the slots with a riffler.

On the top of the base, chisel out a ⅛ -inch-deep section to hold the leather intake valve. Then attach the leather valve with three screws (Figure 8-43). The leather piece lifts up on the upward intake stroke (Figure 8-44), allowing water to flow into the barrel of the pump. The leather piece is forced down, shutting the valve, on the downward stroke. As well as drawing in water, the upward stroke forces the water out of the pump and into the hose. Returning to the barrel, measure the exact length you need and mark the bottom edges of all four sides with a square. The cut through your marks is very important, since a close fit with the base is necessary. Use any hardback fine-toothed saw. (I used a dovetail saw here.) Plane with a block plane and sand with medium sandpaper.

Drill the holes in both cap and base so you can attach them to the pump barrel. Countersink the holes for the cap. Check the fit by putting the screws into place before bedding. Bed *only* the base at this point, thus installing it permanently (Figure 8-45).

Figure 8-39. The cap (left) and base (right) of the pump.

*Figure 8-40. Lines in the bottom of the base are sawed about 1/4"
deep.*

Figure 8-41. The base is clamped securely as the underside is removed with a chisel.

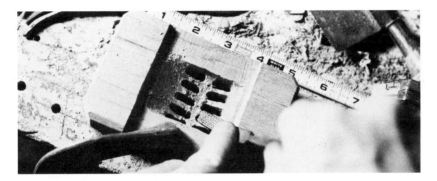

Figure 8-42. Slots in the bottom of the base have been placed off-center, leaving room for attachment of the leather intake valve on the top of the base.

Figure 8-43. The leather intake valve is screwed into place on the top of the base.

Figure 8-44. The intake valve is open on the upward stroke of the plunger.

Figure 8-45. The pump barrel, complete with cap and base. Only the base is attached permanently at this stage; the hole for the rod must still be drilled in the cap.

HOSE CLAMP

Using a bow saw, cut the four-inch-square hose-clamp block in half, and plane off the saw marks. Clamp the pieces back together, draw a circle centered on the joint and slightly smaller than the hose diameter, unclamp the pieces, and cut out the two halves of the circle (Figure 8-46). A circle 1⅜ inches for a 1½-inch-diameter hose allows for a gradual, more precise fit for the hose. Using a No. 11 gouge and finishing with a riffler, cut spirals in each block to fit the coils of the hose (Figures 8-47 and 8-48). The hose will never pop out of place!

Drill two holes on one side, countersinking them deeply to receive 1½-inch screws. Bed all surfaces and then screw the clamp around the hose. Plugs may be hammered in without glue to make dismantling easier, should it become necessary.

Cut a hole in the barrel large enough to receive the hose, bed the hose clamp block, and secure the clamp to the barrel with two two-inch screws. Again, plugs can be hammered in without glue (Figure 8-49).

Figure 8-46. A bow saw is used to cut a semicircle in one half of the hose-clamp block.

Figure 8-47. To hold the hose securely, the insides of the hose clamp are gouged out in a spiral pattern with a No. 11 gouge and finished off with a riffler.

Figure 8-48. The clamp is fitted around one end of the hose. The insides of the clamp have been gouged out to hold the hose securely.

Figure 8-49. The final appearance of the hose clamp.

BRASS PLUNGER AND HANDLE

When constructing the pump plunger (Figure 8-50), keep in mind two facts: the sizes of the rods are important and the holes drilled in them should be positioned exactly. Drill a hole in the main rod to receive the ¼-inch rod. Soldering provides extra strength in case the fit is not perfect. Drill holes in the ¼-inch rod to receive the ⅛-inch rod (or copper nails). Drill a hole in the leather piece slightly larger than the ¼-inch rod; the leather acts as a wedge.

At this point you have a beautiful pump barrel with a very bare-looking brass rod emerging from its cap. Wood or brass can be used to construct the pump handle, but brass seemed logical for me because I had a few pieces left over.

Cut six pieces of brass as follows (Figure 8-53):
2″ of ¼″ stock (continuation of the plunger shaft)
2 ¾″ of ¼″ stock (handle)
1 ⅛″ of ⅜″ stock (stop)
1″ of ⅜″ stock (cap to plunger shaft)
1⅛″ of ⅜″ stock, two pieces (caps to the handle)

Drill six ¼-inch holes as follows:
(a) 1⅛ inches into the shaft to receive the continuation piece;
(b) through the stop;
(c) and (d) ⅝ inch deep in the ends of each of the handle caps;
(e) ¼ inch deep in the plunger cap; and
(f) through the plunger cap to receive the handle.
Drill a ³⁄₁₆-inch hole in the end of one handle cap to allow for dismantling.

The order of assembly of the pump handle (numbers refer to Figures 8-53 and 8-54):
(1) Place 2-inch piece in shaft. It has to be forced because the hole is exactly the same size as the rod (brass piece no. 1).
(2) Place the stop on the shaft (no. 3).
(3) Place the cap on the shaft (no. 4).
(4) Put the 2¾-inch piece of the ¼-inch stock (no. 2) through the shaft cap to make the handle.
(5) Put caps on the handle (nos. 5 and 6).
The bilge pump is now complete (Figure 8-55)—the last of the special projects that enhance your boat and make it truly your own.

Figure 8-50. The bilge pump's brass plunger.

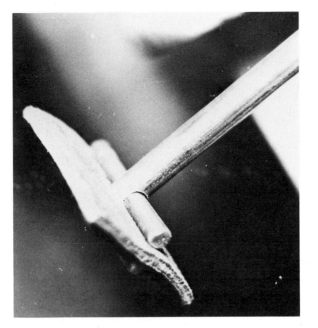

Figure 8-51. The brass plunger with leather exhaust valve. It is now ready to be inserted into the barrel of the pump.

Figure 8-52. The plunger exhaust valve is curved to simulate its position on an exhaust (downward) stroke.

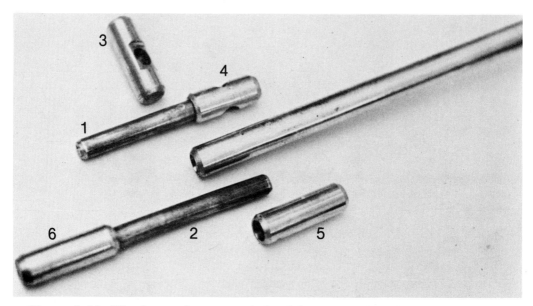

Figure 8-53. The brass elements of the bilge pump handle. Compare with final placement, shown in Figure 8-54.

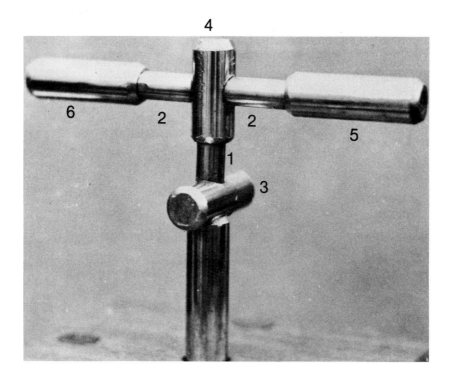

Figure 8-54. The pump handle assembled. Compare with the brass pieces in Figure 8-53.

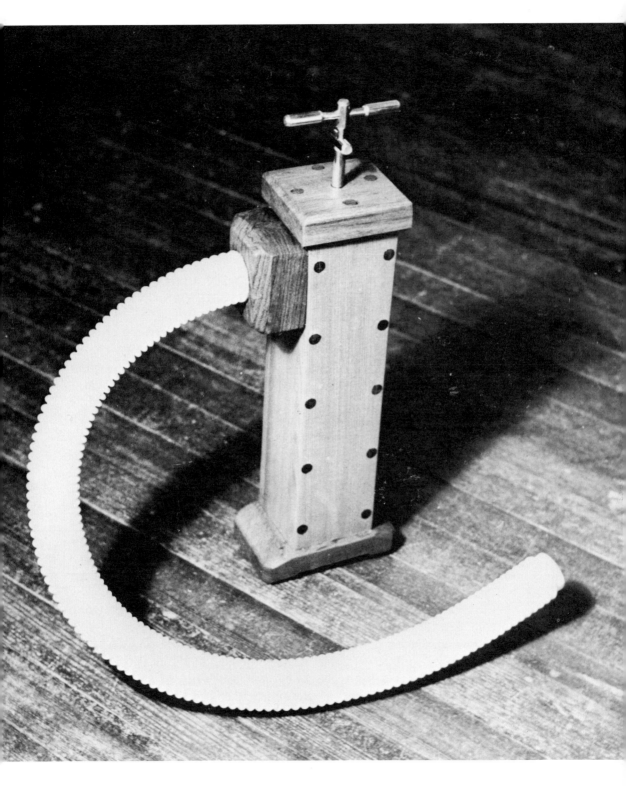

Figure 8-55. The completed bilge pump.

APPENDIX

THREE BOAT DESIGNS BY JOHN ATKIN
WITH NOTES AND COMMENTS BY THE DESIGNER

On the following pages are the designs of three rather diminutive, but amazingly burdensome, flat-bottomed boats, the *Cabin Boy* (in a rowing version), the *Flipper*, and the *Nina*. The smallest of the fleet is the *Cabin Boy*, so well illustrated and described in Clemens Kuhlig's text.

There can be minor departures from the working drawings—all of which is fair enough. The essential requirement is to loft, or redraw, the lines full-size and follow these closely—and to maintain the weight of scantlings. Little boats depend on their liveliness by being light but strongly built.

The use of laminated breasthooks and quarter-knees is most acceptable, providing a *proven* waterproof glue is used in assembling them. In days past, "natural crooks"—from the apple, cherry, or larch tree—were used in these areas. They still have a great deal to offer but are often difficult to come by.

In building the *Cabin Boy,* Clemens Kuhlig fitted the plywood bottom first, then planked the topsides, covering the exposed edge of the plywood. Other builders of this design have let the plywood land on the chines and lower edge of the topside planking. I think the Kuhlig method has a lot to be said for it, but, as in so many matters pertaining to boatbuilding, if the particular procedure followed is done well, the results will be satisfactory. There is, by the way, a lot to be said for using waterproof plywood on the bottom of a small skiff that will be exposed often to the weather for extended periods. As a matter of fact, any of the three boats could very well be built entirely of waterproof plywood, with some consideration given to the weight and thickness of this material.

134

Cabin Boy, Flipper, and *Nina* are three very similar hulls whose designs are based on numerous very successful boats developed by my father and me over the years. Any of these will come up to the expectations of the builder. A well designed, flat-bottomed hull has a lot to be said for it—most all good. It is reasonably simple to build; initially stable; dry; rows and sails exceptionally well; and will be tolerant of a modest outboard engine hung on its stern—but it mustn't be too big!

Complete building prints of the three boats include their lines; offsets; construction plan, elevation, and sections; outboard profile and sail plan (if any); and interior arrangement plan. Scantlings are lettered on the drawings. These are drawn to a large scale in a clear, professional manner and are available from John Atkin, P.O. Box 5, Noroton, Connecticut 06820.

FLIPPER

MAST - SITKA SPRUCE
15'-4" FROM SHEER -
TAKE BURY FROM WORK.

15'-4"

14'-0"

55 ☐

7'-3"

8'-0"

A simple jib-head rig will make the Flipper *a handy sailing boat. She will be ideal for a father and young son or daughter to "learn the way of little boats."*

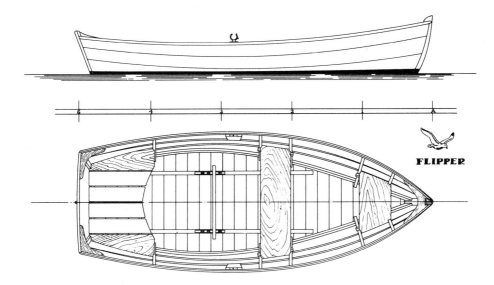

FLIPPER

The Flipper *is a modification of my late father's skiff* Mable, *designed a good many years ago. Freeboard has been increased considerably, but in other respects the design is basically similar. Principal dimensions are 10 ft. ½ in. overall by 3 ft. 11 in. beam and 3½ in. draft. The* Flipper *is an excellent rowing boat and runs extremely true and straight.*

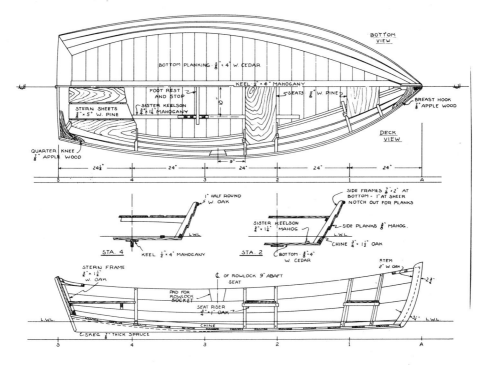

Construction plan, elevation, and sections of the 10 ft. ½ in. flat-bottomed skiff Flipper. *Apple wood is indicated for her breasthook and quarter-knees and will prove most handsome—but these may be laminated of spruce or oak and still prove entirely practical.*

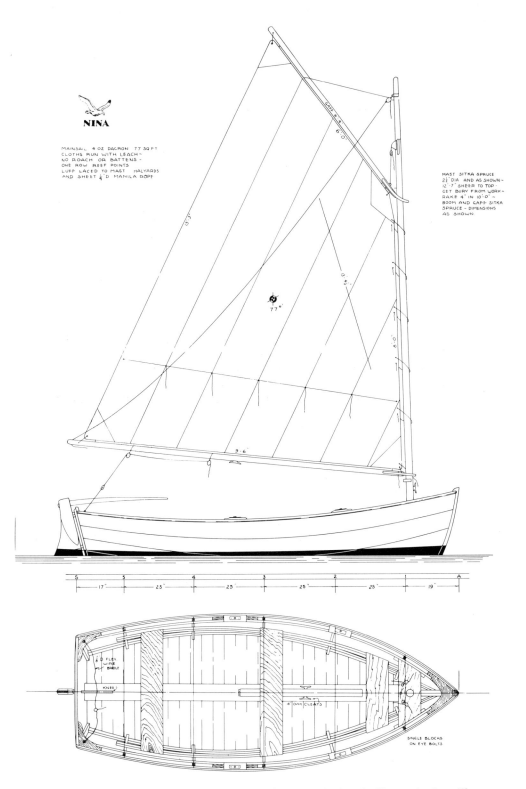

NINA

MAINSAIL 4 OZ DACRON 77 SQ FT
CLOTHS RUN WITH LEACH~
NO ROACH OR BATTENS ~
ONE ROW REEF POINTS
LUFF LACED TO MAST   HALYARDS
AND SHEET ½"D MANILA ROPE

MAST SITKA SPRUCE
2¼" DIA AND AS SHOWN~
12'-7" SHEER TO TOP ~
GET BURY FROM WORK~
RAKE 4" IN 10'-0" ~
BOOM AND GAFF SITKA
SPRUCE ~ DIMENSIONS
AS SHOWN

The Nina's *gaff rig suits the simplicity of the hull, and the "low-aspect ratio" ties together with the balance of her character. She is 11 ft. 4 in. overall by 4 ft. 7 in. beam and 4½ in. draft. While the* Nina *will row nicely, she is more ideally suited to sailing—and should the wind peter out, she can be urged home by an "ash breeze."*

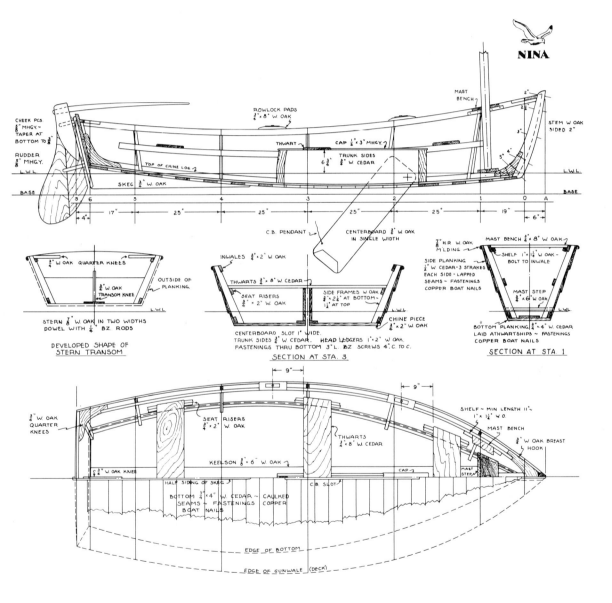

The Nina *is the largest of the three designs—long proven by a lineage of similar flat-bottomed boats. Her construction follows traditional standards, for there is a lot to be said for all vessels based on tradition, proven in the past, for use in the present.*

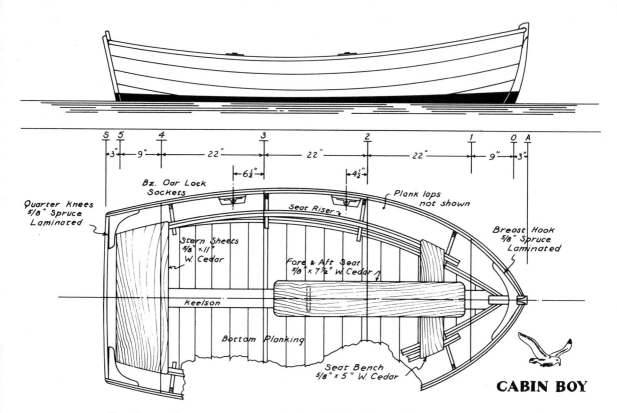

Profile and arrangement of the Cabin Boy. *The seat extending fore and aft is most practical, in that it allows for easy distribution of weights using either set of oarlocks. Bottom planking extends athwartship and should be laid with relatively narrow widths.*

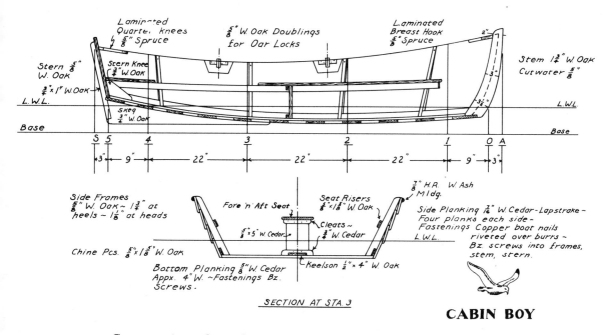

SECTION AT STA. 3

CABIN BOY

Construction plan, elevation, and section of the rowing version of the Cabin Boy. *She is 7 ft. 6 in. overall by 3 ft. 10 in. beam and draws 3¾ in. Waterproof plywood is a practical substitute for her bottom.*